An Assured Understanding

&

Other Sermons

Neville Goddard

Copyright © 2017 Merchant Books

ISBN 978-1-60386-743-6

Contents

An Assured Understanding

n Paul's letter to the Colossians, he said: "I strive for you to have the riches of an assured understanding and the knowledge of God's mystery of Christ." Now, you may think there is no mystery to Christ and believe - as any Christian believes - that Christ is Jesus, the son of God; but Paul doesn't state that. What Paul is trying to do is change your fixed ideas of the past, in order for you to have the same assured understanding and knowledge of God's mystery of Christ that he has.

Paul tells us that Christ is our human life. Now, if you took all of your experiences throughout all of the generations and condensed them into a single youth, it would be David. It is he in whom the Christ-seed flows. This is the same David who was anointed by the Lord and told that he would bring forth a son who would become the Lord's son, being one with the Lord. In other words, David will bring forth a being who is his Father. That is the mystery.

Housed in you, a human being, is the Christ-seed, which will bud and flower into fulfillment as Jesus the Lord. Until David is formed in you, you can describe Christ in many ways, but "No one can say 'Jesus is Lord' except by the Holy Spirit." This is true, for the Holy Spirit brings to your remembrance all that you were told in the beginning.

To understand this, let us look at the parable of the prodigal son. In the story, the one who remained at home complained, because when the son who entered the prodigal state returned, the father killed the fatted calf, and gave him the robe and ring. He was given shoes for his feet and much was made over him. Then the father said: "Son, all that is mine is yours. It is right that we should make merry and be glad for this your brother was dead and he is alive, he was lost and is found."

May I tell you: before you entered this world of tribulation and death you were God the Father, but you did not know it. You had to come into this experience in order to know that the world is yours and all within it. And, since it is all the Father's, the only way you can know it is all yours is to become the Father. You could own the earth, but if you did not know everything in it was yours for the taking, you could die of starvation, not knowing how to appropriate it.

Before you came into this world you were, but you did not know that you were, so you were unaware of all that you owned. Leaving the awareness of being, you came here and became lost, as your consciousness wandered from state to state. But when your journey comes to its end, you will return to your heavenly awareness. Then the Father will embrace you and place his robe and ring of authority upon you. You will be given the fatted calf, which is a symbol of abundance. Shoes will be placed upon your feet to designate your freedom, for only slaves go without shoes. Then that which is personified as humanity will stand before you to reveal your Fatherhood.

This is not spelled out in the scriptures, but - as Blake said, (and he was quite the student of the scriptures): "That which can be made explicit to the idiot is not worth my care." The prophets and the apostles wanted to rouse man's faculties to act. They did not spell everything out, so that man would dig and find the seed within himself.

Every child born of woman contains this incorruptible Christ-seed which possesses the power of self-expression and self-development. And every man is destined to mature and become his own father. If you come out of humanity, then humanity is your father; and if the symbol of humanity is David, and you come out of David, then he is your father - but not forever. Having planted the Christ-seed in humanity, in time it will bud and flower and bring to fulfillment all that was contained within it. And when humanity has done his job completely, you will look back to see David - he who fathered you in the world of time - standing before you and calling you Father. Then you will have matured, for you will have become your own father's Father. That is the mystery of Christ; for the Lord, speaking through his prophet Samuel, told you that when you are gathered together and lie down with your fathers, "I will raise up your son after you who shall come forth from your body. I will be his Father and he shall be my son." Coming out of your body, he seems to be your son, but he is the one who is made to say: "My Father is he who you call God, for I know my Father, as he and I are one."

Everyone will one day discover that he is God the Father, whose son is humanity, brought into focus as a single being called David. I hope you understand, as I cannot spell it out any clearer. I am telling you of my experiences of scripture. I am not manufacturing them, adding to, or speculating about them, but explaining scripture as clearly as I possibly can; for I, like Paul, strive for you, that you may have all the riches of an assured understanding and the knowledge of God's mystery of Christ.

The term, "God's mystery of Christ" is used to express both the human race and the individual who attained the ideal David represents. The human race certainly is not ideal. It is scattered and always at war, but when the race is finished, its experiences are brought together into one single, beautiful being. While humanity is scattered its beauty cannot be seen, but at the journey's end all of its horror is brought together and personified as a glorious youth called David, the son of God, who is God himself.

It was God who buried himself in humanity, and at the end God comes out of humanity. Coming out, he is humanity's son; but when David appears, he is God's son, revealing his father. When that Christ-seed blossoms and fruits in you, individually, you will share the fruit of your labor by telling everyone who will listen to you of the mystery of Christ.

You will notice in the prodigal son story that it was the second son who went out. It's always the second son. Cain killed Abel, the second son. Isaac, Abraham's second son, was offered in sacrifice to the Lord. Then we are told that the Lord loved Jacob, the second son, and hated

Esau. It is said that Judah fathered the twins of Tamar, who - when the first one came out - the midwife put a red string around its finger for identification; but when he pulled the hand back the second son, Perez, came out. Read the genealogy of Jesus and you will find all of these second sons recorded there, for that second son is not a child which comes out of the womb of a woman, but the choice of God. You were chosen by God before the foundation of the world. Then you came out that you may know you are one with God and that there is nothing but God.

No matter how many billions of us there are here now and how many more will come, there are many who are left for a future age. They will come out eventually, but we will all be back as God the Father before we decide on another venture into the world of death. You are blessed because you are the second son and beloved by God. In the state of Jacob, God told you: "I am your inheritance." How will you know this is true? You will know it when God's son calls you Father, for when he does, you inherit God.

The story of scripture is the most fantastic, incredible story you can ever hear and accept. Can you believe that you will become your own father's father? It's incredible, but true, for that is exactly how the Book of Matthew begins: "The book of the genealogy of Jesus Christ, the son of David, the son of Abraham." Now, this genealogy is turned around, for the Bible is based upon a peculiar reversal of order. All through the Bible the second becomes the first, until the very end, when you find yourself coming out of humanity. Then humanity congeals and forms itself into a single being and stands before you and calls you Father.

I came out of humanity, for I came out of this garment of death and was born from above. Five months later I saw humanity -fused into a single being - stand before me and call me Father. Then I knew I had experienced that state in order to join the heavenly being called Jesus, the Lord. Now I am one with the personification of all those within whom the Christ-seed has erupted and flowered into fruitage, for David, the personification of the sum total of all humanity and their experiences, called me Father.

Dwell upon this and you will find David, he who was anointed with the destiny of lordship. Samuel was told to "Rise and anoint him." Taking the holy oil, he anointed David in the midst of his brothers, and from that day forward David never lost a battle. Although David did everything man is accused of doing, the Lord never condemned him because David was always doing the Lord's will. It was the Lord who said: "I have found in David, the son of Jesse, a man after my own heart who will do all my will." Everything is the will of the Lord. "As I have willed it, so shall it be. As I have purposed, so shall it stand. My spirit will not turn back until I have executed and accomplished the intents of my mind. In the latter days you will understand it perfectly."

In today's paper I read where the mafia (whoever they are) wanted to sell the A&P stores a certain detergent, and when A&P refused, two managers were shot and over a period of two years their warehouses were burnt, costing the stores over $50 million. One young twenty-year-old lad was caught. He was used as the front man, while his bosses, with their billions, remain hidden. This is what is known as approximate causes. The young man will be judged and sentenced for a job he received $100 for. But in his mind's eye he was proud to serve those who were so mighty.

You may wonder what good can come out of that experience, but it will. Time will prove everything is good, for all things work for good to those who love the Lord. There isn't a thing that the Lord cannot resolve, because he is the master artist. That which you and I judge as discord will be resolved into perfect harmony. Then one day every experience will stand before you, collected into a single youth whose beauty is so great you cannot believe he could be the sum total of all of the horrors you have gone through. David is the personification of the human race and his beauty is indescribable. And who is his father? I AM.

So, when the question is asked: "What think ye of the Christ? Whose son is he?" they answered: "The son of David." Then he inquired: "Why then did David in the Spirit call him Lord? If David thus calls him Lord, how can he be David's son?" In the ancient days a child always referred to his father as "My lord." When David stands before you, he is standing in the presence of one called Jesus and calls you: "My father; my lord."

Like Paul, I am telling you who I am, and yet you do not understand. But now I am going to my Father and your Father, to my God and your God, for I and my Father are one. Remain where you are now until you are clothed with the power to understand the things I have been trying to tell you, for I strive for you that you may have all the riches of an assured understanding and the knowledge of God's mystery of Christ.

I have shared God's mystery of Christ with you this night. The word "Christ" is used as the human race completely personified in the ideal form as David - and also of the individual who realized that ideal. Everyone in whom that ideal is realized becomes one with the one and only Jesus. The minute God's mystery of Christ is realized in you, you are the Lord Jesus, even though you still bear your present identity, and those who know you by your given name will continue to see you as their friend. But when you take off this garment it will be for the last time, for you are the Lord Jesus. And while you are here you can put your garment down in what the world calls sleep and - as the Lord Jesus - do your work by stirring those whom you have drawn unto yourself, into a quickening state.

Night after night I try to open your eyes so that you will not continue in the sleep of death. Then I return to this garment called Neville and pick it up again because of my obligations in this world. Every night I enter that wonderful awareness, but I know my true inheritance will not be mine until I take off this garment of flesh for the last time. Then without loss of identity I will be one with the Lord Jesus.

You came into this world for the purpose of knowing what you possess. It was given to you, but you did not know it and cannot know it until you leave your heavenly home to enter the world of death. The son who remained was told: "All that is mine, is yours. It is fitting that we should make merry and be glad, for this your brother was dead and is alive, he was lost and is found." Unable to take the challenge, the eldest son remained with the father and served him well in his own wonderful, unconscious way, just like the functions of your body serve you in their own unconscious way. Right now, what you had for dinner is being digested, assimilated, built into your body as bone, tissue and blood. What you cannot assimilate the body will unconsciously expel from your system. It's all part of you, yet playing their unconscious roles. You and I came out to play conscious roles in the body of God, and that conscious role is to be God himself, for there is only God awakening and the awakening will go on forever. There was a limit as to how many he would bring into this world of tribulation and death at any one time. They are measured by the number of the sons of God which he chose in himself before that the world was.

Everyone is destined to discover the fatherhood of God within himself. He will know this when humanity forms itself into a single being and calls him father. Every human part one could ever play, when summarized, is David - that one being you will one day come out of to be born anew. Then, having matured, you will realize he is not your father but your son; for David, in the Spirit, will call you father.

I hope this is becoming clearer to you, for it is so important that you understand the distinction between the two uses of the word "Christ." He is not only the one in whom the ideal was attained, but is humanity which contains the ideal in the form of a precious, incorruptible seed. That Christ-seed contains within itself the power of self-expression and self-development, and will germinate, bud, and flower into fulfillment in you. Then the sum total of all of your human experiences will stand before you in all his heavenly beauty and call you "father."

The story of Jesus is an acted parable to instruct us. When Paul realized this, he said: "O foolish Galatians, who has bewitched you; before whose eyes Jesus Christ was publicly portrayed as crucified. Are you so foolish having begun with the spirit are you going to start worshiping some little being of flesh? Did you receive this understanding by works of the law, or by hearing the story with faith?" Well, the Christian world has ended with the flesh. They see Jesus as a body of flesh and blood, even though he tells us in the Gospel of John: "I and my Father are one and my Father is Spirit." If you and your father are one and your father is spirit, are you not spirit? Are you who began as spirit going to end as flesh?

Today the entire Christian community worships a man of flesh and blood. But like Paul, I will no longer see any character of scripture as human; even though I once regarded Christ from the human point of view I regard him thus no longer. Now I see the entire Bible as an allegory. Paul puts it quite clearly when he says: "The story of Abraham is an allegory." As a devout Jew, Paul thought Abraham, Isaac, and Jacob lived as men after the flesh; but when his eyes were opened he saw all scriptural characters as backgrounds - spiritual eternal states that culminate in the one in whom the ideal blooms. Then he knew he could not see the blooming ideal as flesh, when all the others are spirit. All of the characters in scripture are eternal states of the spirit through which the immortal soul passes and comes to that final state called Jesus, when the seed called Isaac which was planted in you in the beginning of time, comes to fruition. You will find that the second son is always sacrificed - Abel, Isaac, Jacob, one after the other, culminating in the one grand being who is God himself.

I hope I have made it clear tonight, for I strive for you that you may have all the riches of an assured understanding and the knowledge of God's mystery of Christ. It is my hope that when you hear the word Christ you will not think of some historical being who lived 2,000 years ago, but understand the great distinction between the two uses of the word: one representing humanity in its ideal form, and the other representing the man from that human race in whom the ideal was attained. Everyone in whom that ideal is attained is Jesus Christ, and you will all know you are he without any loss of identity. That's the great mystery. So, when you read the Bible in the future, keep this important division concerning the use of the word Christ in mind. At one minute you are speaking in the name of the Father, and in the next moment in the name of the son. Learn to discriminate between the two, and you will see how the same awareness is playing the different parts.

You are playing your part right now by doing God's will. You will play it just as it has come out, and as it will be consummated. And remember: in spite of the horrors of the world the end result will be beautiful. You will see this beauty of the summary when David calls you "Father." That was the plan before the beginning of time. In the state of Abraham, we were given a preview of what we would experience, but we did not know that at the end we would become God himself.

How could man believe it, when the son who remained complained that he never once received one kid. He could not understand how, when the one who was so wasteful returned, he was given the fatted calf, the robe, and the ring, and shoes were placed upon his feet. He was told, but he could not understand.

Many years ago, I had a vision to illustrate this point. I came upon an enormous sea of sunflowers, each with a human face and each flower rooted in the earth. When one swayed, they all swayed. If one smiled, they all smiled. They moved in unison, while I - certainly not as beautiful as they - knew I was freer than any of them. Not one could detach himself from that ground. Not one could frown if the others smiled. Not one could stand erect if the others bent over, for everyone moved in unison. They were the sons who never came out. But I, having left my heavenly home and gone through hell up to that vision, knew I enjoyed a freedom they could not conceive of. I was free to walk among them, smile, laugh, cry, and bend over, while they could not do one thing independent of the other. They did not know that everything was theirs for the taking. But you who have gone out from the Father will return to the Father as the Father, knowing that everything is yours. Then you will understand that 50th Psalm: "If I were hungry I would not tell you, for the world is mine and all within it. The cattle on a thousand hills are mine. Were I hungry I would slay and eat." Why ask any man's permission to use that which belongs to you?

This is the story of scripture, but man is unaware of his inheritance until he is born from above. From then on, he will not be concerned with making an effort to bring his desires into reality; he will know they already are real.

But until that day, apply the law towards any desire of your heart by assuming you have it. Sleep as though it were true and it will be drawn to you. Keep on applying the law towards these many ends until the Christ-seed bursts into bloom. And when it does, your fleshly body will come off for the last time for you will know you are the Lord Jesus. No one can say that Jesus is Lord except by the Holy Spirit, and when the Holy Spirit comes he will bring to your remembrance all the things that I have told you by re-enacting the drama within you.

Having seen the preview of the play before the journey began, when the end comes you will enter the play to discover you are God the Father.

Now let us go into the silence.

An Inner Conviction

I tell you that imagination creates reality and I ask you to imagine a state, any state, which would imply the fulfillment of your desire. It doesn't really matter what anyone else thinks; it's what you think that matters to you! If you create a scene which implies the fulfillment of your desire and dwell in it until you have an inner conviction that it is real, what does it matter what another thinks?

In the Book of Habakkuk (which means "to embrace") the prophet speaks to the Lord as: "Thou who art of purer eyes than to behold evil." Then he asks the question: "Why are you silent when the wicked swallows up the righteous? I will take my stand upon the watchtower, to see and hear what people say to me and what I will answer." Now the Lord speaks, saying: "Write the vision plain upon the tablets so that he who runs may read it. For the vision has its own appointed hour; it ripens and it will flower. If it be long, then wait, for it is sure and it will not be late."

There are those who try to rush everything into being. They try to force birth from conception, but it cannot be done. There are many experiences not recorded in scripture, and I am not here to stand in judgment of anyone as to whether they have experienced scripture or not. But I do know from experience that on this level, if you dare to assume you are what you want to be, your inner conviction, your feeling of certainty will bring it to pass. When you embrace the desired state, you have assumed its impregnation, and its fulfillment has its own appointed hour. It will ripen and flower. If the state is slow in objectifying itself wait, for it is sure and will not be late.

I know that when I was told I could not get out of the island of Barbados for at least six months and I desired to leave immediately, I assumed I was walking up the gangplank of the ship. I felt the dampness of the rail and tasted the salt air of the sea with the feeling of certainty that I was leaving for America. I made that gangplank so real that I hadn't even broken the spell before the phone rang and I was offered passage for the following week. Although I had been told that I was on the bottom of a list of over two thousand names, my family and I were singled out to board that ship. So, I know that the truth of any concept is known by the feeling of a certainty, a peculiar knowingness that it is true.

You can take this same concept into all levels of your being, for any desire is a concept. You can move into any desire and express it. Ask no one if you are entitled to it or if you did it - only you know what you did. It happened to you. Now wait for the vision (the desire's fulfillment) for it has its own appointed hour. It ripens, it will flower. If it seems long then wait, for it is sure and it will not be late.

Returning to the overall picture of God's rising in Man, let us go back to the Book of Exodus, where we are told: "The time that the people of Israel dwelt in Egypt was four hundred and thirty years. And at the end of four hundred and thirty years, on that very day all the hosts of the Lord departed from Egypt. It was a night of watching by the Lord." Then Moses is told to keep this night in memory.

Scripture teaches a mystery. "Great indeed is the mystery of our religion." The word "mystery" is defined as "a religious truth revealed by God that man cannot by reason alone discover." Here is a doctrine of revealed truth.

We are told in the 15th chapter of Genesis that "You and your descendants will be enslaved for four hundred years." Now, the number four hundred is the twenty-second letter of the Hebrew alphabet whose symbol is the cross. Your body (of beliefs) is the cross referred to as four hundred, and as long as you wear it you are enslaved in a land that is not yours. But in the end, you will be brought out with great possessions!

In the 12th chapter of Exodus, thirty years has been added to the four hundred, and in the New Testament it is said that Jesus began his ministry when he was about thirty years of age. In this world you are enslaved, and here you remain playing your part until you are embraced, impregnated, and thirty years later Christ is born in you and your trials and tribulations are over! So, four hundred does not mean years, but thirty does. Four hundred records the length which Blake calls 6,000 or 8,500 years. Call it what you will, it is the period of time man plays his part in this world. Then comes the moment when, as Man, you are selected, called and embraced, and told to stand upon your watch; for the sign has its own appointed time to ripen and to flower, and that time is thirty years!

My friend, Benny, does not remember the embrace, but I remember it well. It was in 1929. I was fully aware of the embrace, just as I was fully aware of its fulfillment in 1959, so I can tell anyone from my own experience how it happens, but I can't tell you when if you cannot remember the embrace. Only after impregnation can I prophesy as to what, and when these things will come into being.

But I do know that God's law reflects all the way down to this world of Caesar. I do not know how long it takes for each egg to hatch in a nest, but I do know each one will hatch in its own time. And so, it is with an assumption. If I desire to be wealthy, I may not know how long it will take me to reach the conviction that I possess great wealth, but when I feel wealth is mine I have conceived. Conception is my end. The length of time between my desire and its conception depends entirely upon my inner conviction that it is done. A horse takes twelve months, a cow nine months, a chicken twenty-one days, so there are intervals of time; but it comes down to the simple fact that the truth concerning every concept is known by the feeling of its certainty. When you know it, not a thing can disturb your knowingness!

In my own case, as I felt the gangplank under my feet and the salt mist on the rail of the ship in Barbados, the phone rang and passage was mine. There have been other times when it has taken longer. Unfortunately, we do not keep an account to see how long it takes to come about after we have done it. But a concept is an egg and remains so until occupied. Occupy your desire! Feel its certainty and you can prophesy its fulfillment.

Although I did not know what would become of it, I kept a record of what happened to me in 1929, so when I was born from above and raised from within myself in 1959, I looked back to discover that it was thirty years. I discovered that Jesus began his ministry when he was thirty years of age, and that Israel made their exodus thirty years after the four hundred recorded in Genesis. We are going to celebrate this exodus in the immediate future as the Passover, "a day to keep in memory forever." For "this is a night of watching by the Lord. On this day the Lord will bring the entire host of Israel out of the land of Egypt" and they will come out one by one. So, if someone tells me a story that is not part of my experience, I cannot confirm it or deny it; I only know that my experiences parallel scripture.

But I say to you: everything has its own appointed time. It ripens and will flower. If fulfillment seems long, wait, for it is sure and will not be late. Everything comes on time, but we do not know the time interval because we do not record the conception. In my case, I keep a diary. I check scripture to find out where the passage is that I have experienced and record the date beside it. Now I know the length of time it takes to fulfill scripture. I also know that when it comes to the world of Caesar, I have received confirmation while in the silence. I have exploded right into the now and, having felt the thrill I knew it had to happen, but I did not know when. It could be a day, a week, or a month. Three weeks ago, I heard good news for a friend, and today I received confirmation that it was completed. I will not catalog that event to say that particular desire equals all desires, because a desire can be as different as a chicken's egg is from the egg of an elephant. I do know, however that events of scripture do have definite time periods. Scripture fulfills itself in God's time, and you cannot delay it or hasten its coming.

A friend wrote me this week, saying: "I found myself sitting at a table looking at a beautiful plate containing a raw steak, when I heard the words, 'Eat it'. Obeying the command, I then heard voice say, 'You have eaten the body of God.'" This lady has fulfilled the 51st to 56th verses of the 6th chapter of the Book of John: "My flesh is the bread of life. He who eats thereof has eternal life." She has completely eaten the body of revealed truth and eternal life is now hers. I cannot tell her when she will be called, but she has accepted the revealed truth, which is the body of God.

Another letter came, telling of how this lady spent the day working on her husband's books. She was so very tired that as she fell asleep, she said: "Father, I cannot take every aspect of the day and change it, but I can imagine that it never happened." So, she began to create a scene which would imply that all the problems of the day were resolved, when out of the nowhere she saw an enormous scene of mountains clothed with magnificent trees. As she watched, she discovered that her mental activity caused the trees to move. And that the world pictured on the outside adjusted itself to be in harmony with her thoughts. Then she said "I came to the conclusion that my God is a God of action, for I saw everything I was imagining taking place now. I feel as though the world is moving in me like being on parade." That's how God sees Man. We are forever adjusting to his perfect being. He is looking out, yet everything is taking place within.

Tonight, I ask you to take the most fantastic thing in this world and find an inner conviction within yourself that it is yours, for the truth of any concept is known by the feeling of certainty which that conviction inspires. Once you have that inner feeling of certainty, don't ask me to confirm it. What would it matter what I think? Do not be disillusioned if your experience has not been mine. Believe in yourself and trust your inner feeling. Test yourself and if it works on this level it will work in the depths of your being.

If, in my imagination I climb a gangplank, and as I look with nostalgia at the little island of Barbados and the phone rings, offering me the passage I desire, am I not influencing my outer world? Was the phone call not reflecting my mental activity? I arrived at the point of feeling a peculiar certainty, and that certainty was its inspiration.

You can always tell the truth of any concept by the feeling of certainty which it inspires. When you imagine seeing the world as you desire it to be and are inspired as to its truth, it doesn't matter what anyone else thinks. I don't care what it is; when you know what you want, you can make your desire so real, so natural that you will reach a feeling of certainty which no power in the world can stop. When that feeling is yours, drop it. Don't ask anyone if what you did was right or wrong; you did it and that's all that is necessary.

Now let me share the letter I received from Benny. He said: "Friends of mine (Negroes), a man and his wife, invited me to a party. On the way we stopped at their home, where a group of Caucasians in their teens were having a party. Suddenly my friends appeared in the doorway, coat and hat in hand, and said, 'You stay and mind the children.' I was shocked, but turned to look at the boys and girls, when out of the nowhere a blond, blue-eyed, fair skinned lad came toward me, and as I looked at him I knew he was David. He looked me in the eye and said, 'I know that our Father will never leave us.' At that moment I knew my son David, yet I also knew I fathered them all. This was on Wednesday. The following Friday as I told this experience to my friends, I awoke to discover that I had been dreaming, for I awoke on my bed."

Here is the doubling of a dream, the confirmation as told us in the 41st chapter of Genesis. Now, you cannot violate the story of scripture. David is described in the 16th chapter of 1 Samuel, and you will not change this description no matter who you are. The Christ child is not described, for he can be black, pink, white, or yellow. There is no description of Jesus either, but I will tell you who he is. He is the Ancient of Days as described in the Books of Daniel and Revelation. When you see David, he is the youth of the ancient one he observes. Benny is now wearing a very dark skin, but in the eyes of his fair skinned, blond and blue-eyed son David, Benny is the Ancient of Days, the Holy One of Israel. The one we recognize and call Benny now knows himself to be the Risen Lord. Now I will tell him that on the 8th day of July he will be split in two from top to bottom. I know, for the vision has its own appointed hour, it ripens, it will flower. If it seems long, wait, for it is sure and will not be late.

Now the Book of Ezekiel begins: "In the thirtieth year the heavens opened and I saw visions of God." Ezekiel gives you a day and a month, meaning nothing. The important thing is that in the 30th year the heavens opened and visions of God were his. "And as I looked, behold, a stormy wind." That's exactly what happens. An unearthly wind comes in that thirtieth year, and you are born from above, born anew through the resurrection of Jesus Christ from the dead. Jesus Christ is God's pattern of salvation buried in you. His death in the most literal sense is your life, and his resurrection is possible only after he impregnates himself.

God the sender and Man he sent are one. Falling in love with the one he sent, God impregnates him. He plants his seed, which takes thirty years to germinate and is his mission to start. This experience comes to Man after he has borne his cross in this wilderness world for thousands of years. In spite of the horrible things that take place in the world, when the individual is called and embraced, what does it matter what he has to go through before he awakens? In a short period of only 30 years he will be born into an entirely different age, for during that time he is taken out of this age and placed in that age, the age of the kingdom of heaven.

Now, because you know this concept, don't feel that you are better than someone else, you are creative power. Stand upon your tower and watch to see what God will say and how you will answer. Do this by assuming you are the person you want to be and seeing what you would see if your assumption was real. Remain there until you feel its certainty, until you reach the point of satisfaction, until you are convinced of its truth; and although the world may collapse around you, you will become that which you have assumed you are.

In the 21st chapter of the Book of John it is said that if all things were told concerning Jesus Christ, the world itself could not contain the books; so, do not think that because I have not had your experience, that it is not true - but do not try to force me into accepting it. Believe what you choose and go your way this night. My pattern has followed scripture completely, from the embrace to the descent of the dove, but I am not saying it is the only way.

I am saying, however, that you can be the man (or woman) you want to be, but not by simply wishing. You must make the effort to look at the world mentally and see it reflect your fulfilled desire. And when it does you must remain in that state until you reach the inner conviction that what you are seeing, touching, tasting, smelling, and hearing is true, clothe yourself in the feeling of its reality - and explode! Do that and you are pregnant. And what do you do after pregnancy? Nothing! You simply wait for its birth to appear in its own appointed hour. And it will! When you least expect it, your desire will objectify itself in the world for you to enjoy, whether it be health, wealth, or fame. That's how God's law works.

Now, to the one who had this experience the other night, I know you are anxious to give it birth right away, but what is thirty years in this fabulous eternity? You were awake when it happened, and you will never lose its memory. Should you depart tonight to find yourself a young lady of twenty, you would only be fifty when you brought forth the Christ child. Then you would see the complete pattern fulfill itself in three and a half years and enter a new age, which is the world of eternity. My dear, you are destined to know departure from this world of death and entrance into the world of eternal life as you move from darkness into light. But your reaction was natural.

It reminded me of a story I heard in New York City. This young girl came rushing into the subway, and standing in front of a gentleman she said: "Would you please let a pregnant lady have your seat?" Jumping up, terribly disturbed, the gentleman said: "When is the baby expected?" And she replied: "I don't know, it just happened." But this lady knows it will be thirty years, but what is thirty years when you have been called, you have been selected, you have been chosen. You are one of the elect!

Now let us go into the silence.

Awake, O Sleeper

he Bible is addressed to the Imagination - which is spiritual sensation - and only immediately to the understanding, or reason.

In the fifth chapter of the Book of Ephesians we are told to: "Awake O sleeper and rise from the dead." Now, reason could never comprehend these words, but the Bible is calling upon Imagination to awaken, telling Him that he is sleeping, dreaming his world into being. But Imagination, now a rational being, does not know this and therefore cannot believe it.

All of the commands of scripture are addressed to and fulfilled by the Lord, who is all Imagination! It is your own wonderful human Imagination who is called upon to "Rouse thyself! Why sleepest thou, O Lord? Awake!"[1]

The greatest confession of faith man has ever received through revelation is called the Sh'ma. It is recorded in the 6th chapter of Deuteronomy as: "Hear O Israel, the Lord our God, the Lord is one." The Lord spoken of here is the Elohim, which is a compound unity of one, made up of others. I know, for I have stood in His presence. He embraced me and incorporated me into His body. Since that day back in 1929, I have been one with the body of the Risen Lord.

I believe we are the gods spoken of in the 82nd Psalm, which is quoted in the tenth chapter of John as: "God has taken his place in the Divine Assembly. In the midst of the gods he holds judgment, saying: 'You are gods, sons of the Most High, all of you; nevertheless, you shall die as men and fall as one man, O princes.'" You will notice that this statement begins in the past, claiming men are gods, sons of the Most High. Then the future is prophesied as: "You will fall as one man."

---

[1] Psalms 44

This fall was not a punishment, but a plan - a pretense by an assumed appearance in order to conceal the real intention, which is an expansion of further existence and ultimate birth! Having chosen us in Himself before the foundation of the world, one man fell, fragmenting itself into the unnumbered men that now appear. We are the gods in disguise who do not recognize our brothers, or ourselves.

In the beginning of Genesis it is said: "The Lord God caused a deep sleep to fall upon man, and while he slept took one of his ribs. God made a woman from the rib and brought her to the man who said, 'This at last is bone of my bones and flesh of my flesh; she shall be called Woman, for she is taken out of Man.' Therefore, man must leave his father and mother and cleave to his wife, as they become one flesh."

This statement is myth when viewed through the eyes of reason, but it is true. You will understand it perfectly when it is revealed in you.

Having had the vision, I say you have no body distinct from your soul. The body that scripture calls Eve is a portion of the soul discerned by the five senses. The physical body you wear, be it male or female, is emanated by Eve. She is the Jerusalem from above, who is the emanation of the Lord.

Although hidden from view, you are so one with Eve that if you were struck and felt pain, you would proclaim, "I am in pain," and I am is God's name. Imagination is joined to you and you are joined to me by our emanated Jerusalems. The Jerusalem from below bear's sons into slavery, and the Jerusalem from above bears sons into freedom.

When questioned by the Jews, Jesus said: "Destroy this temple and in three days I will raise it up again." Not understanding, they said, "It has taken us forty-six years to build this temple, and you will raise it up in three days?"

That's how the mind of man thinks. Thinking of an external thing made with human hands, they did not know that Jesus was speaking of the temple of the soul. Paul knew this, for he questioned the

Corinthians, saying: "Do you not know that you are the temple of the Lord and the spirit of God dwells in you?"

Eve is your temple, your emanation, and your wife till the sleep of death is past. She is your soul, which God (Imagination) cleaves to and has become one with. There is no other Eve.

Falling in one body, you entered your cave and met your savior in the grave. Some found a female garment there and some a male, woven with care. I found a male garment. My wife found a female garment, but she is not female and I am not male, for in Christ there is no male or female, no bond or free, no Greek or Jew, no black or white. Being one with Christ, you - all imagination - are above the organization of eternal death.

In his great work called "Jerusalem," Blake speaks of the sleep of Albion and his passage through eternal death - which is life as we know it. This world seems to be endless and without purpose, for when a rich man dies, he leaves his wealth behind. And when a poor man dies he is placed in a pauper's grave. But given the same length of time, their bodies will turn into dust and bones, and no one will be able to distinguish one bone from the other.

Regardless of what man seems to achieve here, the wisdom of this world is foolishness in the eyes of the Lord. And the strength of man here is the weakness of God. Yet this world has purpose, for man has to pass through it in order to enter into eternal life.

In Blake's poem, "Jerusalem," he tells of the sleep of power as it passes through eternal death, and of its awakening into eternal life, saying: "This theme calls me in sleep night after night and every morn awakens me at sunrise. Then I see the Savior over me, spreading his beams of love and dictating the words of this mild song."

In his letter to Mr. Butts, Blake spoke of this poem, saying: "I can praise it because I dare not pretend to be anything other than the secretary whose authors are in heaven. It's the grandest poem this world contains, for the spirit of truth dictated it morning after morning, sometimes twelve, sometimes twenty or fifty lines at a time.

What now seems to be the labor of a long life was produced without labor or study and quite often against my will."

This is how the poem begins: "Awake! Awake O sleeper in the land of shadows, wake! Expand! I am in you and you in me, mutual in love divine."

The being in whom we were contained deliberately fell into this state called death, for the purpose of expansion into glorious life. His story is told in the parable of the grain of wheat, which unless it falls into the earth and dies, it remains alone. But if it dies, it brings forth much. Here is the story of the mystery of life through death. Being all Imagination, if I want an extension of reality, I must contract and die. I must empty myself of the glory I had with the Lord, and enter the one body, which falls.

The world tells us the fall was a mistake but that is not so, for God planned everything as it has come out and as it will be consummated. One day you will awaken, your mask will come off, and you will be enhanced beyond your wildest dreams as you awaken to eternal life. And when we all awaken, we will know each other more intimately than is possible to know one another here. My wife and I often think the same thoughts; but no matter how intimate we may be, we cannot know the intimacy that will be ours when these garments are taken off and we are once more awakened into eternal life.

Everyone will awaken in time, but not by any effort on their part while here. Your awakening was predetermined and it will happen on time, regardless of whether you are shining shoes or employing a million people. Our government undoubtedly has a million people on its payroll, with the president as its head. So, in a technical sense he employs a million; yet tonight the one who shines his shoes could awaken, while the president continues to sleep, yet no one can die. That is the glorious part!

Your body is your emanation. Cut off its head and - believing you are it - you will instantly renew the same body, but with no missing parts. You will step out of the garment you now wear and men will call you dead; but you will have just stepped into another garment with no bridgework, no fillings in your teeth, no gray hair, no need to wear glasses or a hearing aid, to discover you are a young man (or woman) about twenty years of age. You will be in a terrestrial world just as real as this one, and continue your journey until you awaken.

I have awakened and know that when this garment is taken off I will no longer be in this world of death. This world, however, does not terminate at the point where the senses cease to register it.

You cannot follow those who are called dead, because of your limitation. But your friend who emanated the body you knew here is not dead to himself. Rather, he now emanates the same body, only young, where he continues to dream his world into being, not even knowing that he has gone through the door called death.

It's like leaving one room and entering another. Your friend is in the same fabulous, terrestrial world which the mysteries call eternal death, and from which he will one day awaken into eternal life. Having descended and entered the world of death, one day he will awaken to discover he has expanded and fulfilled his purpose. God made a limit to contraction and opacity, but not to translucency or expansion.

In the 1st chapter of Genesis it is said: "God made man in his own image. Male and female made he them." The 2nd chapter changes this somewhat, but it is not a contradiction if you see it through imagination.

"The Lord God formed man of dust from the ground and breathed into his mouth the breath of life, and man became a living soul."

Man's destiny is to become a life-giving spirit, not just to remain an animated body. The purpose of your fall is to transform you into an entirely different world, one where you are a life-giving spirit, animating everything around you. There you will stop time at will and start it again. That is your destiny. Now, reason cannot understand this, and you can't blame anyone who has not had the vision. Scholars believe the Bible is all myth, and certainly it is. If you take my body apart you will find no rib that is missing, yet scripture tells us one was removed.

The word rib is the Hebrew word "tselah," (TSAY-la), which literally means, a portion of the soul that emanates, that leaves everything and cleaves to his emanation until they become one flesh.

You have cleaved to and become your emanation so completely you believe you are it. When you introduce yourself you always say, "I am" before you give your name. And if you are hurt you say, "I am in pain." Always calling upon the name of God, you don't say, "God is in pain," but "I am," and that is God's name forever, because the gods came down.

Now let me repeat: I not only believe in God, I believe that all men are gods and that collective Man is God. I believe that when you hurt men, you hurt God. And when you hurt men you hurt yourself, because you are God and there is no other.

In spite of the horrors of the world, God is love! When you stand in His presence you can't feel anything but love. And when love embraces you and you become one with God, you will know an ecstasy you have never known before. And with this union, you are incorporated into His body and know yourself to be all love!

"He who is united to the Lord becomes one Spirit with him."[2] When you are incorporated into the body of love, you are united with the one body, the one Spirit, one Lord, one God and Father of all, knowing that you are He. Then you will awaken as the one who commanded the fall, for you will have fulfilled your purpose.

You will awaken in this world of death knowing you are God, the Father of God's only begotten son, David. It is recorded that in the spirit David called Jesus "Adonai", which is the Hebrew name for Father (Lord). (In Hebrew the name YAD HE VAU HE (pron. "YOD HEY VAV HEY" is so sacred the word "adoniyah"[3] is substituted.) In the spirit, David will call you father, and you will have fulfilled the 2nd Psalm. It is David who says: "I shall tell of the decree of the Lord. He said to me, 'Thou art my son, today I have begotten thee.'"

---

[2] Romans 6

[3] corr. adonai, pron. "a-do-NAI"

One day when your time here is fulfilled, you will awaken and be born from above. Then David will appear and the entire drama of scripture will unfold within you, revealing your true identity. Then you will know you are one of the gods who agreed to dream in concert.

Now dreaming in concert, you and I see a building identically. You may see it through the eyes of one who would like to own it. I may see it through the eyes of one who admires it with no desire of possession, but we see the same building. We see the same streets and recognize the same number so we can go where we want to. But the world is a dream and we are the gods who agreed to dream in concert in order not to have any confusion. Had we agreed to dream individually and all play solo parts, this would be the wildest, maddest play possible!

I invite you now to go all out and imagine you really are the man or woman you want to be. But do not doubt, for the minute doubt steps in, a mental division descends, as doubt is the devil. If you will believe that regardless of what the world tells you, you are the man you want to be, you won't go mad. Instead, you will become that man. Your dream world will rearrange itself to fit your new image into it without any difficulty or help on your part.

When someone born into poverty persists in dreaming he possesses great wealth and his dream comes true, his wealth seems perfectly natural to those who do not know his dream. You are dreaming. If you try to make your dream come true while doubting its possibility, you are heading toward a nervous breakdown. But if you go all out in your wonderful claim, you will fulfill it, for all things are possible to the God you are, for you are the God of whom the Bible speaks.

When the gods came down in the likeness of men, some found a female garment and some a male. Entering death's door with those who enter, and lying down in the grave with visions of eternity, the gods are dreaming the dream of life until they awake and see Jesus and the linen clothes which were woven with the cooperation of a male and female. These were emanations of the soul which is neither male nor female.

"As it was appointed for all men to die once and after that comes the judgment, so Christ was offered once for the sins of many and will appear a second time, not concerning sin, but to save those who are eagerly waiting for him."[4]

You may hear of someone's death, but he has not died to himself, as it was appointed that all men would die only once. We died when we left our heavenly home to come down and assume the limitations of the flesh. At that moment we were united with Christ in a death like his, with the promise that we would be united with him in a resurrection like his.

Your death is over. When you go through the gate called death, you don't die, but instantly emanate a young, unaccountably new body. Most of those who go through the gate do not even know it. They simply take their young body for granted, just as they do everything here.

All day long a miracle goes on in your body. Unknown to your conscious reasoning mind, tonight's dinner is being converted into blood, tissue, and bones. No man can make a drop of blood, grow a new heart, or make one hair on his head.

The other day it was recorded that a doctor had stated that his patient could not live three weeks without a heart transplant. He operated on the man, gave him a new heart, and the man lived 18 days! No matter what the doctors do, no man will live one hour beyond his span of time as told us in the Sermon on the Mount. "Who by being anxious can add one hour to his span of life?" Yet man goes blindly on believing he can. All he is doing is publicizing his surgeons and the medical world. You are not the body you wear, so when its heart, liver, or lungs wear out, you will simply step out of it and emanate a new one.

Made in the image of God, you are God's prodigal son who came out from the Father. You have cleaved to the body you wear so tightly, you have become one flesh with it, so that whenever it is hurt,

---

[4] Hebrews 9

you are hurt. That is the Adam and Eve of scripture, therefore, it is not a myth. Your emanation does come out of you, but not from a rib. You have no body distinct from your soul. Your called body is a portion of soul discerned by the five senses, the chief inlet of soul in this age. You are now a living soul, destined to become a life-giving spirit.

Having fallen, you emanate a body, which is necessary to function in this world, and you automatically do it with not one part missing. I meet those who have left this time/space and do not even know they have died.

If I told you right now that you are not only sound asleep but you are also dead, you would think me mad and the possessor of a demon. That's what they said of the Risen Christ. "Why listen to him, he is mad and has a demon." Taking up stones to stone him they said, "We stone you for blasphemy, for you being a man claim you are God." Then he replied, "Is it not written in your law, 'I say you are gods?' If he calls you gods to whom the word of God came, then why do you say of him whom the Father consecrated and sent into the world that he blasphemes?"[5]

Jesus never claimed he was greater than another. Those who heard him did not know they were God, and he was only trying to awaken them to the memory that they were the sons who came down. He said: "Go tell my brothers that I am ascending to my Father and your Father, to my God and your God."

He never claimed that his Father differed from theirs or that his God was different, but they could not understand the mystery. They tried to grasp it with the reasoning mind, yet everything takes place in the Imagination, which is God. "Man is all Imagination and God is Man and exists in us and we in him. The Eternal body of Man is the Imagination and that is God Himself."[6]

Now let us go into the silence

---

[5] John 10
[6] William Blake

Barabbas Or Jesus

onight's subject is "Barabbas or Jesus." This is the greatest trial that ever took place in eternity. You have read of trials in countries where billions are involved. It means nothing compared to this trial. This is the greatest of all trials. When we read the scriptures, we find things like the raising of Lazarus, which is the most fantastic thing you can imagine. A man who was dead for four days and his sister said: "By this time there is an odor" and he raises Lazarus, and yet only one Evangelist records it - only John tells the story. Matthew, Mark, and Luke do not mention the story of Lazarus. How could you tell the story of a man in this world who could raise someone who had decayed and bring him back to life, as we understand life, and not tell it as part of his biography? I could take you through the many stories and show you that one story is told by two, and sometimes three, and only by one, but here, in this story of the trial, all mention it. It has tremendous significance. The story of the greatest trial that ever took place in eternity.

May I tell you: it is taking place here tonight and you are the witnesses. You are the ones who will either cry out for the release of one or the other. It is entirely up to you, for this is the story; it must take place in this manner. The supreme effort of God to reveal himself in the present tense was the coming of Jesus. Jesus came to reveal God as the eternal contemporary. That is the trial. One believes it or they disbelieve it. But here is this supreme effort to reveal himself in the present tense - for the present tense is "I AM," - that is my name forever. I have no other name.

Let us turn to John 18:38-40. Here a man is on trial. He knows who he is, for he has had all the experiences to reveal the being he is - sent into the world to tell the world who he is and to tell them who they are, for they are one. He is brought to trial and Pilate - the arm of Caesar - is trying him. And Pilate said to him: "What is truth?" but he does not reply - he does not answer. Pilate said to the crowd: 'I find no crime in him. But you have a custom that I should release one man for you at the Passover; will you have me release for you the King of the Jews'? They cried out again, 'Not this man, but Barabbas!' Now Barabbas was a robber.

"Barabbas was a robber." That is all it states. "Not this man, release Barabbas." Well, here is the trial. Who is Barabbas? He is only mentioned in one little statement, but in the four gospels. It is very significant.

To find out who Barabbas was, let us find out who the thief and the robber is in scripture. We go back to John 10:1: "'Truly, truly, I say to you, he who does not enter the sheepfold by the door but climbs in by another way, that man is a thief and a robber.'" They did not understand it. He said to them: "I am the door of the sheep."[7] There is no other way in to this sheepfold.

Now you present the case to the world. Will you believe it? Will you believe as you are seated here tonight, regardless of your present limitations, that the only door in to your success, in to your future as you would conceive it or desire it to be, there is only one door, and that door is "I AM"? There is no other door into that sheepfold? And if you go through that only door the sheep will hear your voice, they will recognize your voice as the shepherd and will respond and come out? I would like to be healthy if I am unwell at the moment. I would like to be gainfully employed if I am unemployed. I would like to be - and you name it -to be happily married. I name all the things that I think would constitute a lovely life in your world. Do I really believe there is only one door into that sheepfold where I could bring all these unseen things out into my world? And these things could only respond to the voice of the shepherd - and the shepherd is "I AM"?

And so, he asked the crowd and they shouted out: "Release Barabbas." They would not have Jesus released - they would have

---

[7] John 10:7

none of it. So, they chose the robber and the robber rules over them to this very day. That is the world. I chose the robber. My senses rob me of all that I could be. I see my bank balance - and I know the world as my senses allow it. I know what reason dictates in my world and yet I want to be other than what they dictate. Yet I can't bring myself to believe the only way into that sheepfold is by the only door in the world, and the only door is "I AM."

So, here Jesus comes to reveal God in the present tense, and man refuses it. They speak of God in the past - "He was" or "He will be," but few people in the world can believe in the reality of "I AM," and that is the great trial, and you are on trial tonight because you are asked the question: "Will you believe that your own wonderful I AM-ness is the one and only God?" Or: "Do you believe, because of your present social, intellectual, or financial position that you are less than someone else?" and you allow your reason to dictate this as something that is final? Can you believe tonight in this trial and really believe that I am - - - and you name it - - - and dare to believe it?

I could tell you unnumbered stories where it has worked - if people would believe me. In this audience tonight there sits a man - only a few weeks ago he was let out of a job. I told him it would make no difference to me if he was let out and they told him it was forever, that it was permanent - that I would hear good news for him, good news. So, I heard exactly what he would tell me were it true, and tonight, just before I took the platform, he told me he has been transferred to a new job where his income is in excess of what it was before. All things being relative, when you make $13,000 on a job, that is not hay. Yet, it could be $100.000, and I am telling you right now I don't care what he has ever done in the world today exceeding $13,000; it could easily be, if that is what he wants.

There is only one door into the sheepfold and that door is "I AM." The supreme effort that God ever made to reveal Himself to us in the present tense came through Jesus. So, Jesus comes affirming God as the eternal contemporary, forever and forever. If tomorrow you have a child or a grandchild, they are going to say, "I AM." It is contemporary - forever contemporary, and eternally contemporary. It wasn't that he was - it is always "I AM." And so for one to declare, "I am" - and simply name it and sleep as though it were true - there is no power in the world that could stop it.

Now this is one level to this fantastic trial. There are numberless levels to this trial. First of all, the word "Barabbas" means "son of a father." Jesus means "savior." For every child born of a woman is the child of a father. "Bat" usually means "daughter" and "bar" means "son." They are interchangeable depending on the context. So, Barabbas is now known as "son of a father." And they chose the son and denied - it does not say the father, but I will show you how they denied the father, for Jesus said in the same Gospel of John: "When you see me you see the father. How could you say, show us the father? He who has seen me has seen the father." So, he declares "I am the father."[8]

"'I am the way, and the truth, and the life; no one comes to the Father, but by me.'... Philip said to him, 'Lord show us the Father, and we shall be satisfied.' Jesus said to him, 'Have I been with you so long, and yet you do not know me, Philip? He who has seen me has seen the Father.'"

Now they deny the father to fulfill a prophecy.[9] "They will put you out of the synagogues; indeed, the hour is coming when whoever kills you will think he is offering service to God. And they will do this because they have not known the Father, nor me." For there is a prophecy that when a son destroys the enemy of Israel, the Lord will set his father free. They didn't choose the father to set him free - they set the son free. The one that is robbing them morning, noon, and night, they set free. "And the men of Israel said, 'Have you seen this man who has come up? Surely, he has come up to defy Israel and the man who kills him, the king will enrich with great riches, and will give

[8] John 14:6-9
[9] John 16:2-3

him his daughter, and make his father's house free in Israel.'"[10] The father of one who destroys the enemy. His name is "I AM," called "Jesse." The word Jesse, the word Jehovah, the word Jesus - are identical in meaning. They mean simply "I AM." I will set that being free - and his name is "I AM."

Now, if tonight you could do what dozens or hundreds of you have done and believe this is not a little trick - it always works - and really believe in it, you would believe in God. When a lady sits in this audience and is in her seventies and has no money and dares to sleep in a home in need of repairs; and she looks at the unrepaired, unpainted house and she could smell paint and could see the whole thing as it would be seen were it true that things were exactly as she wants it to be, and she sleeps in that assumption - what is she actually saying? If I said to her: "Who is smelling anything?" she would say, "I am smelling paint." "What are you seeing?" "I am seeing a repaired house." "What else?" "I am seeing that the whole thing has been paid for." She falls asleep in assumption of seeing from her own wonderful center - I am seeing it - I am smelling the paint - all these things she is doing and in one month it was all repaired and painted and paid for, with a surplus of $7,000 - a gift from one she had never seen in this world - only communicated with her two or three times in the course of a year. Here, she saw it.

Her story I told in my latest book. She may have even forgotten the name of God. Who did it? She may point across the water to a lady in England, 8,000 miles away, who died and left a certain will where she received $7,500 in U.S. currency, which allowed her to do all these things with something left over. She might think the cause of it all was one who died - and I tell you the cause of it was: she called on the only name of God in this world. She went into a sheepfold through the only door in the world, and that door is "I am." She fell asleep in her bed, but before she fell asleep she saw and could smell paint and she saw the repaired areas all painted over and felt herself

---

[10] Quoted from 1 Samuel, 17:25

giving a check in full payment for all the work done. Because it was fun she did it for nine or ten days and then came this wonderful draft from England and a letter from Lloyds Bank telling her of the story. She entered the sheepfold and they all heard her voice and they all came out. The sheep happened to be the money. Everything in the world responded to her voice. She was calling them out - she was calling out paint, calling out the repair job, calling out everything. They only responded to the voice of the shepherd.

Who is the shepherd? "I AM" the shepherd. There is no other shepherd. If you think he will shepherd you, and put your trust in our President (or our mayor, or our governor, or your father or mother or some uncle who is about to die, and you are now giving the most marvelous meal in the world because you think he is going to leave you in his will, so he is your shepherd, and all these you think are the shepherd) you are simply looking in vain. There is no other shepherd and no other door into eternity save the one door, and that one door is "I AM."

Here is the greatest trial that ever took place in eternity and you are called upon to scream out the one you want released; and the world invariably screams out (but not all, there is always that minority who will scream out, "Release Jesus") but the majority will scream out, "Release Barabbas!" Release the robber! And so they chose the robber, and throughout the centuries the robber has ruled over them right down to this day. You and I will go to bed tonight and our senses will dictate what we ought to believe to be true in this world.

Read this morning's paper and ninety-nine per cent, including the ads, were all paid for. And if it is something you like, you will buy it. It is perfectly all right. It has been paid for and you know it. But you don't know all the news items were paid for also. That has been concealed. They are all paid for. All the press agents all over the world - there is not one who is in the public eye that does not maintain some press relationship, daily columns - not press agents. They have been glamorized into some name other than "press agents." But still they take your money month after month and put these little items in the story and you read it morning noon and night and you believe that to be true. I tell you: forget the entire vast world and ask yourself a simple, simple question: What would I like to be? Look at the world. Forget Cuba, forget Russia, forget China, forget all this stuff that is going on in the world. What would I like to be? A decent, wonderful being that contributes to the good of the world? To be happily married? Yes - to be in this world and contribute to the good of the world - but really contribute, so that when I am gone and my children's children are gone, they will say: "He gave a thought to the world that has fed the world." The unborn tomorrow could be fed by what I have left behind me. Would I like to do that? At the same time not neglecting my obligations tonight, for I am married - there is a husband, a wife, a child, a father, a mother - all these things in the world, and I must, if I love them as I think I do, take care of them. And so I want enough to leave them cushioned. Regardless of all things they did not need my cushioning, but maybe they didn't hear me, and I am selfish enough that if they did not hear me there is only one door in the world into the great kingdom - if I could still leave them a cushion so that they will be cushioned against tomorrow's blows. Then regardless of what the world tells me, I will assume tonight that I am what I desire to be and dare to fall asleep in the assumption as though it were true. I will actually believe in it. So I will cast my vote: "Release Jesus" and hold on to Barabbas." Or else I will say: "Release Barabbas, and hold onto Jesus." And, so it is entirely up to us. I either believe it, or don't believe it. The one called Jesus - his name is "I AM."

Now let me quote from Galatians 4:13, 14: ". . . and you know it was because of a bodily ailment that I preached the gospel to you at first, and though my condition was a trial to you, you did not scorn or despise me, but received me as an angel of God, as Christ Jesus." It is Paul speaking. He says, when I came to you I was a trial to you, yet you accepted me. And then one little phrase divides the thought. We will omit the phrase: "You did not scorn or despise me, but receive me as Christ Jesus." He is telling you who he is. You accepted him, now you are going to turn back like those in the desert who disbelieve. And then he said: "You observe days, and months, and seasons, and years! I am afraid I have labored over you in vain."[11]

Here we are in what is called "a season" - the Lenten Season - and then we have another season and another month. A few years ago, we had the Marian Year, and all this goes all the way back. "You observe days, and months, and seasons and years! I am afraid I have labored over you in vain." That man could turn outside of himself (and the whole thing has been revealed to him, who he really is) and believe in the sacredness of a certain day or a certain month, or season, or year! He is trying to tell the whole vast world who he is, and they received him as Jesus Christ.

There is only Christ; there is only Jesus. Jesus Christ is God, and so are you and so am I. If I believe it, I am it; even if I don't believe it, I am it. If I don't believe it then I go through all the fires of hell in this world. If I believe it, there is no being in this world that can stop me from sleeping this night in the assumption that I am the man that I would like to be, just as though it were true. I will bring it to pass in my world because I call all my sheep out and my sheep are the individual realities. No one sees them. They come right out and follow the voice of the shepherd whose voice they hear. They will not obey the voice of the stranger, only the voice of the shepherd. And the shepherd is "I AM."

So here is the greatest trial in the world and you are the one to judge. You sit as though you sat in a jury and you bring in your verdict. And he rises and asks those who hear the testimony - "It is customary" - and may I tell you there is no evidence as far back as man can go to support this claim. No scholar or historian can find any such custom where there was an amnesty at Passover, it is only attested to in scripture. So you can see it is a play; it is a fantastic

---

[11] Galatians 4:10

play, and here is the play and at every moment of time the play is taking place.

"It is your custom that I release to you one man. Would you have me release the King of the Jews?" - for he is the King of the Jews - and who is he? Jesus. Who is Jesus? "I AM." And so are you and so is every being in the world. That is Jesus and his name is "I AM." For the name is one with Jehovah. "I and my father are one," as told us in John 10:30: "I and the Father are one." I am one with him. What is his name? "I AM."

There is no other way in, no other door - just one. And so who will you have me release, the King of the Jews, whose name is "I AM," or release Barabbas, who is a robber? A man based purely on the sense of the body. "Release Barabbas!" So, they released the robber and he, to this day, rules them. For man cannot believe, or is unwilling to believe, that something is real that his senses cannot confirm. He must have it confirmed by the senses. If reason allows it or my senses allow it, then I will accept it, but to sleep this night, when unemployed (and I know six million are unemployed and I am not as qualified, as I think they are looking for certain qualifications) and I dare to believe that I am gainfully employed, with more than I ever made before - and go to sleep as though it were true, in the conviction it is true - and then I am employed and it is beyond what I make?

When he told me tonight, I can't tell you my thrill. He will not be here because this takes him away a hundred-odd miles. I say to him: Good! Go and tell it. Tell it to those in your sphere. Tell it to everyone that you meet. If we never meet physically again, it does not really matter. I like him personally, he likes me personally, but the physical contact is not important. We are forever one in eternity, and so he can't get away from me and I can't get away from him. He heard the story and he knows it works. Now go and tell it.

So, here we are at every moment in time, called upon to pass judgment upon the eternal drama - the greatest trial that ever took place. God is on trial and he is presented to the world because the sense man is what he wears and so he presents it. Would you believe in me that you cannot see? For you can't see "I AM." You can see I am a man - that is the sense man. But man cannot believe in the reality of "I AM." Something entirely different.

So, here, this great trial will be presented this coming Sunday (called Palm Sunday) and they will all tell the story of how they placed the palms before him. If you have the Apocryphal Gospel, may I recommend that you read the Gospel of Nicodemus.[12] It is called "Ulsa – one of the acts of Pilate." in fact the title is "Gospel of Nicodemus, or Acts of Pilate." What a fantastic story!

It is all about this trial. I think many of you have James' combination of all the apocryphal books. Why they delete them I will never know, because they add so much to the thought. But here in this story of the great trial, when they placed the little piece of cloth before him as he came in to be tried, and all the standards and all the images bowed before him. They could not believe that this thing could happen. And they did it over and over and over again, every time he is brought in. Every inanimate object bowed before him as he came in the building on trial.

How true that is may I tell you? You will have the thrill of your life one day when suddenly the whole vast world is going to stand still before you and it will be dead - but really dead, and you will look at it and then you will release it and it will move on and you stop it to prove that you truly are life, and life itself. When you read these words: "I am the way, the Truth and the Life," you will know how true that statement is. When he said: "I am the Truth," can't you see what a marvelous thing he is telling us? A true judgment need not conform to the external fact to which it relates. Today I will say what is true concerning my world. Well, I pay so much rent and have an average income of so much, and I have obligations to life, and these seem to be the facts. That is true. I tell you: that is not true. For a true judgment need not conform to the external facts to which it relates. Truth depends upon the intensity of imagining and not upon

[12] N.T. p. 94

facts. So, I will imagine that I am _____ and I name it, that which I want to be, and believing that I am that which I am assuming I am and remaining loyal to the assumption, I become it. I have done it, or I would not be here tonight.

I have actually done it, time and time again. But man will always slip back into Barabbas, the man of sense. He must ever remember the trial and always move out, in spite of all the facts that would deny it. Live in the dream just as though it were true, and no power in the world will stop you from becoming the fulfillment of your dream. But no power! You don't need any other being, because God's name is not "he is," or "she is," or "they are." His name is "I AM." Before you say anything in this world you have to say: "I am." You don't pronounce it. But if I ask: "who are you?" you say: "John," but before you say John, you actually, in the depths of yourself, said: "I am John." Before you said anything you actually were aware of being, and that awareness of being was actually in the depths. I am. That is God. There is no other God.

So, God stands on trial and he will be tried in all the churches of Christendom this coming week, and they will all weep and carry on how God was tried. "And the crowds shouted out: 'Release the thief and the robber'" - one who was an insurrectionist, and they do not know who he is. They will make a mental picture of a horrible beast who was an awful, awful man. That is not the man at all. They are the man. For they are calling to release themselves of sense, and make that the real being in the world, and hold on and deny Jesus. Listen to the words from Acts 16:31: "Believe in the Lord Jesus, and you will be saved, you and your household." The only Jesus that you could ever believe in that could save you, would be "I AM." That is His name. And He has only one name in this world. Jesus simply means, "I AM."

It is spelled yod he vau shin ayin.[13] The root of the name Jehovah is Yod He Vau - the shin ayin put into the name of Jesus, which is

---

[13] *ed.* yod hey vav shin ayain

Jesua[14] is for a definite purpose. Shin is made in three little prongs like this: שׁ"" and it is called a consuming fire, a tooth that devours, that consumes. And ayin is an eye. Were it not for that in the name of Jesus I would have to accept as final everything that I see. But in the name of Jesus - which is called "Savior" - what I don't want I could consume. So, it is yod he vau shin ayin. So the Yod He Vau is the root - that is Jehovah, that is God, that is what I am. But a shin is put into my name and so is an ayin. With a shin, I can just see the world. I don't like the way you look. Don't you feel well? No. Well, then I will consume it. I will see you as you ought to be seen by me and the world, and seen by yourself. Therefore, I actually see you differently. I am consuming what formerly you appeared to be.

And how do I do it? The ayin - it is an eye. So, what is his name when he comes into the world, and how does he operate? Listen to it carefully: When he comes into the world, "He shall not judge by what his eyes see, or decide by what his ears hear."[15] So I see. I go to the hospital, you are dying. Go to see anyone else and you see him - it is fatal, regardless of the nature. They can't get a job - there are too many unemployed - this, that, and the other. There it is, the fact. I will not now judge "by what my eye sees, neither will I decide by what my ears hear." So, what will I do then? I will see what I want to see - then a shin is present. It consumes the former state; it completely consumes the past as it seems to be real, and I will put in its place what I want to see and what I want to hear.

So, they tried to quench the voice of Peter and John and they said what they would do to them if they continued to teach this story. And they said to the Sanhedrin, the great wise men of the day: "Whether it is right in the sight of God to listen to you rather than to God, you must judge: for we cannot but speak of what we have seen and heard."[16]

---

[14] *ed.* Jeshua
[15] Isaiah 11:3
[16] Acts 4:19,20

So, whether you think I should do what you tell me I should do - all right, you judge it. The wise men of the world - called the leaders in politics or religion - they will tell you without vision what you should see and what you should preach. They had no vision - none whatsoever, never in eternity - but they are going to tell you how you should tell the story. So: "Whether it is right in the eyes of God to listen to you, rather than to God, you must judge. We cannot preach other than what we have seen and heard." So, I cannot preach other than what I have seen and heard.

And may I tell you: I have seen this story, and when you see it from afar - it is one man, just one man. As you approach it, it becomes unnumbered races and nations of people. I saw it as clearly one night when Blake asked me to fall backwards and I did exactly what he told me to do to produce the vision. And here was one man, a glorious, radiant man. His heart was all like living rubies. I approached it and moved forward and I fell through space like a meteor. When I came to a standstill, here I saw one man and then with Blake's suggestion I moved forward to this one man - a radiant being. As I came closer I noticed the heart was like a ruby and there were unnumbered, innumerable beings making up the heart, and the whole body was made up of nations and races - the whole body. When I came close enough I recognized myself. I was he, containing within myself the whole of humanity. So, I know from experience that when you see God you will see yourself. At a distance it is one man. As you approach it, it becomes unnumbered men composed of races and nations - all one.

And so, this whole vast thing is the most wonderful play, and the final drama leading up to that very exit from this sphere is this trial. So I hope you will bring in your verdict tonight and your verdict will be: "Release Jesus." But if your verdict is: No, I must accept my senses more than I will accept the invisible reality, then it is your choice. You are free to bring in your verdict. But your verdict will be brought by you. I can recommend the verdict, if you dare to believe in the reality of your own wonderful I Amness, believing that it is God and there is no other God. Listen to the words: "For I am the Lord your God, the Holy One of Israel, your Savior. I, I am the Lord, and besides me there is no savior."[17]

There is no other savior. I am the Lord thy God, the Holy One of Israel - thy savior - and besides me there is no savior. Believe that, and rather die than turn back, and you are moving toward being born from above.

Now let us go into the silence.

Q & A

Question: Is there a fixed guide?

Answer: Well, I believe all of us present here have a certain code of decency, and I would go along with it - but I would put into practice what I told you tonight. I would guide myself with my code of ethics. If you asked me tonight to join with you in knowing someone was dead for your good fortune, I could not. I would not deny you the right to want it, but I would say: go elsewhere. I could not actually dream with you that someone died because you were left in his will. But I would not deny you the right to want such a thing. I would leave it up to your judgment. We all have a certain code and I think anyone who would come to a meeting of this nature would have a code - a code of decency - that I would call a code of decency. I am always right if whenever I use my imagination, I use it lovingly on behalf of another. I am on the right track. So that, to me, would be the guide: is it a loving thing to do?

You have the wonderful statement in the Bible: "Do unto others as you would have them do unto you." It is the simplest code in the world - it is done in the positive manner. "Do" - not: "do not do." (But it is written in the positive in the New Testament. In all other religions, it is written in the negative.) "Do unto others as you would have them do unto you." So, what would I like in this world? Something lovely, something wonderful? Well, do the same thing to

---

[17] Isaiah 43:3,11

anyone in the world and every time you use your imagination lovingly on behalf of another, you have done the right thing. Read Galatians 4:14 - that one little thought in which "as an angel," is superfluous, because the next phrase is "as Christ Jesus." But "as an angel" - it might stop right away. That is all inserted to cushion him, because they actually saw him as the central being himself. He looked upon me as Christ Jesus, but if you put the little phrase before it, "as an angel," that arrests the mind and you don't associate Paul with Christ Jesus.

I tell you: he was the one in whom the whole thing awoke. It was Paul. Everything has to come right out of the Jew. The world will not believe it. It is the most fantastic story in the world.

Now, Bishop Pike, who was born a Catholic and became a priest - he gave it up and became an agnostic; then became a most brilliant lawyer in New York City practicing corporate law. He then rejoined the church as a Protestant and rose in no time (he was only in his forties) to Bishop Pike of California. If you have ever heard him, he is an able speaker. He has a wonderful brilliant mind. Bishop Pike made the statement: "I am a Jew." Remember, he was born and raised a Catholic, became a Catholic priest, gave it up then became an agnostic, became a lawyer, went back into the priesthood, this time a Protestant priest. Now he is the highest in the Protestant world. You can't go beyond that. But he said: "I am a Jew because I am a Christian. I could be a Jew and not be a Christian, but I can't be a Christian and not be a Jew." You think about it. Meditate upon that thought. It is true. The whole thing comes out of Israel. It is a mystery, the most fantastic mystery in the world.

So, I am proud to say I am a Jew because I am a Christian. I have been born from above. I could not possibly be, unless I were a Jew. I know, when the veil is lifted and the whole thing is revealed - well, it is fantasy beyond the wildest dream!

Be Imitators *of* God

"It has been taught us from the primal state, that that which is, was wished until it were."[18]

od started with a wish, saying; "Let us make man in our image." And we are told that we will be perfect as our Father is perfect, and holy as our Father is holy. Therefore, whatever God was, when his work is completed, man must be. We are told to be imitators of God as dear children, so we must discover how he became us in order to imitate him.

It seems God lives as one possessed by a dream. Jeremiah tells us: "The will of the Lord will not turn back until he has executed and accomplished the intents of his mind. In the latter days you will understand it perfectly." God, refusing to turn back, remains lost in his dream until he has executed and accomplished the intents of his mind.

If you want your dream realized, imitate God by becoming totally possessed by your dream. Do this and you, too, will reach your desire's fulfillment, just as God has brought - and is bringing - his dream to completion. Have an intense wish. Clothe it in tones of reality and imitate God by living as one possessed by a dream. Like God, do not turn aside until you have executed and accomplished the intents of your mind.

God began the good work in you and when he brings it to completion on the day of Jesus Christ, you will reflect the glory of God and bear the express image of his person. If God will not stop until that wish is completely realized, then you must be equally persistent.

---

[18] William Shakespeare -

Regardless of things to the contrary, persist until your dream is completely realized.

See the story of Jesus Christ as God's plan of redemption. Read the directions, and you will discover that it is only as the Risen Christ that Jesus makes himself manifest. When Judas asked: "How will you manifest yourself to us and not to the others?" he answered: "Any man who loves me will keep my word and my Father will love him and we will come and make our home with him. He who does not love me does not keep my word for the word I speak is not mine, but the Fathers who sent me.

Scripture is the Father's word. First recorded as individual expressions of the Risen Lord, each vision is complete within itself. With nothing in the paragraphs to indicate their chronological order, the writers wrote a story - which appears to be history, but it is not.

I will take one such paragraph, as it fits a letter I recently received. In it she said: "I fell asleep requesting a deeper understanding when you appeared as the Risen Christ and handed me the number 26. I have tried to understand this and can only come up with the number eight."

If you add the two and the six together you have the number of the Risen Lord. It was on the eighth day (the first day of the new week) that Christ rose; therefore, eight is always associated with resurrection, regeneration, and the number of the Lord. But I gave her the number 26!

There are 22 letters in the Hebrew alphabet, of which five are repeated and called finals. We have kaph as 20, but when used as a final it becomes 500. Mem is 40, whose numerical value becomes 600 when used as a final. Nun is 50, and when encountered as a final it is 700. When peh is first encountered it is 80, but as a final it becomes 800, as its tone does not change. The symbolical value of this letter is the mouth; in its final form it is the mouth of God: "My word that goes forth from my mouth shall not return unto me void but must accomplish that which I purpose and prosper in the thing for which I sent it."

You are Christ, the Word sent forth from God's mouth as his hope of glory. God is making you into his perfect image to possess all that he possesses, as God's Word cannot return void. This is the mouth I have given this lady. Recently she has been wondering why - when she knows something intuitively - she is hesitant to speak out. Questioning herself, she fell asleep and saw me as the Risen Lord, at which time I gave her a voice of authority to speak out, regardless of what others may say.

Only the Risen Lord will be seen. I can tell you: I have ascended from earth and entered the highest heaven, but you will not know it until my Father reveals it to you. When asked: "Who do men say that the Son of man is?" they said: "Some say John the Baptist come again, others say Elijah, Jeremiah, or one of the prophets of old." But when he asked: "Who do you say that I am?" Peter answered: "Thou art the Christ, the Son of the living God." The Risen Lord then replied: "Flesh and blood could not have told you this, but my Father who is in heaven, he has revealed it to you."

Many will tell me they love what I teach, but walk away, not believing it to the point of application. But those who truly love me believe and apply my words. They are the ones who will see me as the Risen Lord. They will recognize a man called Neville - not as a man of flesh and blood, but as a completed pattern; for the pattern which God placed within me, has erupted. If you love the idea of completing such a pattern, then you are in love with me. Not as flesh and blood, but the Christ who has risen within me. When I manifested myself to this lady she knew I was Neville; yet she also knew I was the Risen Christ; thereby, having the same experience as Peter. Having heard and loving the message, Peter recognized the Risen Lord - while others heard it, but - not loving the telling - they did not have the experience. Such is granted through the discernment of love.

Many claim to love Christ, but worship an icon on the wall. Called the image of God, Christ is God's plan, which was in the beginning with God, when he said: "Let us make man in our image." Christ reflects the glory of God and bears the express image of his person.

That image is found in the pattern. I have described this image in a more chronological manner than recorded in the Bible.

I know those who have fallen in love with the story which awoke within me. One who departed last July saw me as the Lord. Another lady here saw me as the Risen Lord. They did not see me as a man of flesh and blood, but as spirit, God's power and wisdom raised out of the physical world and into the kingdom of God. Just as God has deluded himself and lives as one possessed by a dream to bring it to fulfillment, you can imitate him while you wait for his work to be completed in you. And if you are equally persistent in your dream, no power can stop it from coming to fulfillment. But you cannot deviate. You cannot turn from the dream to see what others are doing, or what they think about it; you must be willing to lose yourself, to be possessed by your dream. No man of flesh and blood is Christ. "If any one says: 'Look, here is the Christ!' or 'There he is' believe him not."[19] When Christ comes, it is from within and its knowledge is without uncertainty. No one can ever deny the truth of what this lady saw. The man who stands before you now is full of weaknesses and limitations of the flesh. Tomorrow this lady could hear of some unpleasant happening in my life, but it would not disturb what she saw and heard when - in vision - she saw me as the Risen Lord and I gave her the voice of authority. From now on she will have the courage to speak out when she intuitively knows she is right.

Now, when you experience Christ and tell your friends, 99.99% of them will turn their back upon you, because they will see you as a mortal with human weaknesses, and you will not impress them. But don't share your experiences to impress anyone, rather to show the truth of God's word. Do that, and there will be a remnant who will believe; then you will appear to them as the Risen Christ.

Read scripture carefully and you will discover that no one saw him as the Risen Christ until after the ascension, which occurs while wearing the body of man. I know, for on the eighth day of April, 1960,

---

[19] Mark 13

I ascended; and from that day on everything in me has turned around, although I am anchored here during the day. I have been seen as the Risen Lord in New York, San Francisco, and all over, by ones who are in love with the word which they have heard from me. They love the hope I have held out to them, that in a body of flesh and blood with all of its weaknesses, there is a plan of salvation that will awaken and unfold in all. That plan is the Christ they love.

No man born from the womb of woman is Christ. If there is another Christ other than he who was crucified and buried within you, he is false, and false teachers teach him as another. Christ is God's plan of redemption. "He has made known unto me the mystery of his will which he set forth in Christ as a plan for the fullness of time." Christ is the word who is one with the individual who speaks it.

Imitate God as a dear child, by having a controlled dream. Make a composite picture of what you want. Ask no one to aid you or if it is right for you. Desiring life to be full, do what God does. Make a wish and possess it. Turn neither to the left nor the right, but persist, just as God is doing, and nothing can keep you from expressing it.

Then, when you have finished the work you came to do, you will understand that the furnaces you have gone through were necessary to bring you out as an image who reflects the glory of God and bears the express image of his person, for you will be endowed with life in yourself. Having become one with God, you will have inherited all that God is!

In my book, Resurrection, I have shared my visions in their chronological order. I know of no other book, including the Bible, which has given it that way. The Bible in its manuscript form is a series of paragraphs. These paragraphs were used to tell a story, because those who were eyewitnesses were leaving this world of Caesar, and if the events were not recorded, there would only be an oral tradition and confusion would reign. Luke starts his book saying: "Inasmuch as many have undertaken to compile a narrative of things that have been accomplished among us, by those who from the beginning were eye-witnesses and ministers of the word, it seemed good to me also to write an orderly account for you, most excellent Theophilus, that you may know the truth concerning the things of which you have been informed."

The word Theophilus means one who loves God. Luke is writing his orderly account for the individual who, loving the word, enters the state of Theophilus and sees the Risen Lord.

Now, Luke did not claim to make an exact presentation of the source material, but to present it better than those who preceded him in the telling. He tells us that many had undertaken to compile a narrative, yet we only have four records. John tells us that we must be born from above, but he does not bring any of the symbolism into it. But because of Luke's account, the world has taken the story as fact. Believing that Jesus was born from the womb of a woman, they believe he came in the same normal manner as all children do - with one exception, his mother did not have a husband.

Luke tells the story in its normal state, using shepherds rather than kings (as recorded in Matthew). Today's scholars are convinced that the three kings Matthew speaks of were definitely inserted. The witnesses are three normal people, not kings; and the child is only a sign of your birth from above, which can happen when you are fifty or eighty, and has nothing to do with your so-called appearance in this world. While walking the earth as a normal, natural, individual it happens; and when it does you simply record the event next to the parallel passage in scripture. I ask you now to fall in love with my message of salvation. Christ rose in me. God's son appeared to reveal me as God the Father. All is Self, as there is no other. I AM the being called Jesus Christ. I AM the plan, the Word which cannot return void, for I have accomplished that for which I was sent.

Believe me! Fall in love with my message, and Christ will unfold in you; and you, too, will tell it; and those who fall in love with what you say - in the hope that it will unfold in them - will have the joy of seeing you as the Risen Lord, for in the end there is Jesus only.

Because of the nature of the grace that He bestowed, we have different gifts. There are those who have the gift of the apostle; others the gift of prophesy; some are teachers, healers, or miracle workers. All will differ in the kingdom, but the gift itself is unmerited. It is not your due and cannot be earned. The measure of your gift determines the nature of the part you play in the body of the Risen Lord. All parts are important and good, and the least there is greater than the greatest here.

Those who see clearly - as many of you do - are prophets and are so very high in the kingdom. You are the voice of God Himself! Hearing what is being said from within, you are dictated to by the Spirit of Christ - who is yourself. How much closer to God can you get than to be his voice, than to be his mouth? That's what the prophet is. But he is not granted the right to interpret what he hears and sees. That belongs to another aspect of being.

Start now to imitate God by having a glorious dream of the man or woman you would like to be. Don't ask anyone if it is possible, for all things are possible to God. Don't ask anyone if you should want it, simply claim it. Because there is no death in the true sense of the word; if your desire is not fulfilled here, it will be completed, so start your dream and imitate God. You could be ninety and still have things you want to experience, goals you want to realize, so claim them now!

Personally, I hope you will set your hope fully upon the grace that is coming to you at the revelation of Jesus Christ; but if you have no memory of affluence, and want to taste it here, become possessed with the idea and refuse to become diverted. Whatever your hunger may be, make it a part of your dream.

And dream nobly! Imitate God as a dear child! He started with a wish, saying: "Let us make man in our image," and God has persisted in his wish as though it were true. Do as God has done. Take a wish and persist in believing it is true. Do not deviate; just continue believing in its truth, and in the end you will unveil your wish. You will project it on the screen of space, just as God has unveiled his wish as Jesus Christ.

As a man in whom Jesus Christ unveiled himself, I always thought myself to be the body of flesh, not knowing I was that glorified being who reflected the glory of God and bore the very stamp of His nature. I did not know I was perfect as my Father, yet I had not earned it. That I was as holy as my father, but had not earned it. It was all a gift, because it was my Father's wish that I might possess it, and I did.

Now let us go into the silence.

Bear Ye One Another's Burdens

he Bible is the most practical book in the world. In it we are told that one named Simon carried the cross behind Jesus. The word "Simon" means "to hear with understanding and consent to what is heard." And Jesus is your own wonderful human imagination.

The gospel tells what happens in the soul of Jesus. The events recorded there are seen and heard by none save but Him. Through these experiences He gains the certainty that He is not only the Son of God, but also God Himself. But when he tells his story few will accept it, as his experience of scripture differs greatly from its interpretation by the priests and rabbis. Simon, however, understands what he hears and, consenting to it, he carries the cross.

We are told to "Bear ye one another's burden and so fulfill the law of Christ." Now, the law of Christ is described in the Sermon on the Mount. It is a psychological law, as Christ tells you in the 5th chapter of Matthew, saying: "You heard it said of old, 'You shall not commit adultery.' But I tell you, anyone who looks lustfully upon a woman has already committed the act with her in his heart.'" (The word "heart" and "soul" are synonymous in scripture.)

When you are told in the 4th chapter of Psalms to "Commune with your own heart upon your bed," are you not communing with yourself? And in that communion are you not told that the act is committed? I tell you: the law of Christ is imaginal and you carry His burden, for "Inasmuch as we do it to one of the least of these, we do it unto Him."

Paul, seeing the meaning of Christ, said: "From now on I regard no one from the human point of view, even though I once regarded Christ from the human point of view, I regard him thus no longer." Paul realized that Christ was the pattern of salvation buried in every child born of woman, and did not seek a little Christ, but the universal Cosmic Christ buried in all.

There is only one Christ, so when you imagine, you are imagining Christ. Now, one who hears and believes this is called Simon. It is he who goes out and carries the cross by lifting the burden from the back of the one being who is carrying the entire cross; for every human is a cross, who collectively form the cross the Cosmic Christ bears.

When one hears the story and believes it, he goes out to lift the weight of every cross. Seeing someone struggle to pay rent or buy food because he is financially embarrassed, Simon lifts his cross by seeing the man gainfully employed. He does this because he knows he is doing it only to himself, as there cannot be another. As a psychological act, he represents the other to himself as he would like to see that other, and to the degree he is self-persuaded that what he imagined is true, it will become true.

Simon does not move a cross from one little point in space to another. He goes through life following Christ, as he bears the cross and lifts the weight of mankind. Many a man remains behind the 8-ball because no one ever thought he could be anything other than what he appears to be. Fortunately, I had a mother who, at a tender age took me aside and persuaded me that I was her favorite. She would say: "You will make mother very proud of you, won't you?" and naturally I said: "Yes, mother." I wore long white curls at the time, and she would curl my hair, run her finger up my curl, kiss me, and send me on my way - then call the next one to have his hair curled. Mother told the same story to each of us. It was only after we had all grown to manhood that we discovered what mother had done, but by that time she had accomplished her purpose. She didn't expect us to make a fortune but to be one in whom she would be proud, and in our own separate spheres we all became successful in her eyes.

Many a man is a failure today because no one ever believed he could be otherwise. So, I say to you: if you believe that there is only one being and only one cross, you will lift the cross from a seeming other, and - as Simon - follow your imagination to its fulfillment.

Every child born of woman is a cross, animated by Christ Jesus; so when you lift the burden from an infant or one of many years, you are doing it unto yourself. As you bear one another's burdens you fulfill the law of Christ; for inasmuch as you do it to one of the least of these, you have done it unto me. If you believe me and put your belief into practice, you are bearing the cross. But if you are so engrossed in your own little world that you cannot see another as a projection of yourself, you do not believe me and will not become a Simon. Only as you believe and act, will you bear the cross as Simon, enter the temple in the Spirit, and - finding the child - take him up in your arms and say: "Lord, let now thy servant depart in peace according to thy Word, for my eyes have seen the salvation of God."

Called a little child in the Book of Luke, God's creative power is symbolized as the unveiled arm in the Book of Isaiah. In this wonderful 53rd chapter of Isaiah, the prophet speaks of the unveiling of the arm of God as the salvation of the world. And when the prophecy is fulfilled it appears as though you are betrayed, but I ask you: what did Judas betray? He betrayed the messianic secret of Jesus and the place where he might be found.

A secret must first be heard before it can be told. I have betrayed the messianic secret in my book called Resurrection, so I have played the part of Judas. Having experienced the part of Jesus, I have recorded my experiences so that anyone coming after I have gone from this sphere will know the secret.

The messianic secret is unlike that which the priesthoods of the world believe. Jesus is not a little man who comes from without to save mankind. Jesus comes from within, for He is a pattern, which unfolds in and reveals the individual as the Son of God who is God. Knowing my scripture, when the visions came upon me I searched and found they dovetailed one another. I have shared my experiences with everyone who will listen; and those who hear them with understanding and accept them become Simon, who picks up the cross and eases the burden from the back of the Cosmic Christ.

When you meet someone who is unemployed and take a moment to imagine him gainfully employed, you are Simon. Practice this art daily. Pick up your cross and set everyone free from what he seems to be. That is how you bear one another's burden and so fulfill the law of Christ, which is all imaginal.

If you hear this message with understanding you will go out and fulfill the law of Christ. If you do not understand me you may not agree, but I tell you: this is the most incredible story that can ever be told. You need not have a brilliant mind to accept it. In fact, the more brilliant your mind is, the less chance this concept will be believed, yet I tell you it is true. Everyone who accepts it will one-day experience scripture within himself, for the gospel is nothing more than that which happened within the soul of Jesus, who is Jehovah, who is the Lord, in you.

Jesus is your awareness of being, your I AM. It is He who hears the story and either accepts or rejects it. If you think of a man who lived two thousand years ago when I use the word "Jesus," you will not see the Jesus in everyone; for Jesus is awareness, sound asleep and carrying a tremendous burden as His dream. If you will accept my story, Jesus will begin to awaken as you lift his burden and carry the cross behind your imagination. Simon is first seized, and then the cross is placed upon him as the individual who hears and understands and consents to what he has heard.

If you really believe me you will not pass anyone without doing something to lift his burden. Taking up his cross, you will represent him to yourself as you would like to see him; and to the degree that you are self-persuaded, he will become it, even though he may never know what you did. Things will happen in his world and he will become what you conceived him to be, not knowing who did it...but who did it? Christ, for there is only Christ in the world. You can take no credit in the doing, because you are only doing it to yourself.

As you represent another to yourself as you would like to see him, you are lifting his burden and fulfilling God's law. And when your time is fulfilled you will enter the temple and find the sign of the birth of your creative power as a child wrapped in swaddling clothes. Then the arm of God, who creates everything, is unveiled in you and from that day on whatever you imagine will come to pass - I don't care what it is. I ask you to dwell upon this thought and follow the pattern of Simon. Lift the burden of someone today, and maybe tomorrow you will be able to do it to two. Don't let another remain carrying his burden, because there is no other. Lift his burden from yourself and follow Jesus Christ, your own wonderful human imagination.

The dream of life begins with the call of Abraham, and comes to its climax and fulfillment in Jesus Christ. Everyone must and will experience that climax. Then the curtain will come down and you will leave this sphere to join the heavenly brotherhood, who contemplates this world of death saying: "What seems to be, is - to those to whom it seems to be." Take that one little statement: what seems to be is to those to whom it seems to be. You can assume any state and persuade yourself that it is so, and it will become so. Torments, despair, and eternal death will also seem to be, "But Divine mercy steps beyond and redeems Man in the body of Jesus"; for in the end there is only one body, only one Lord, and you are that one Jesus Christ. You will wear that one Risen Body as your own and be the one Spirit that inhabits it. And you will know yourself to be that one Spirit who is the Lord of all.

Today you are not aware of your true identity, but Paul made it very, very clear in his 2nd letter to the Corinthians, when he said: "If we have been united with Christ in a death like his, we certainly shall be united with him in a resurrection like his." Do you see the difference in tense? We have already died with Christ, and we will live with him when God's pattern of salvation erupts and the gospel unfolds within us individually.

Now, whenever I tell my story there are always those who - knowing me by my physical origin - do not know me by reason of my spiritual birth. Seeing only the outside man called Neville, they judge from appearances and claim I am blaspheming by making these bold claims. But a few will believe me and become Simon by lifting the burden and transforming the lives of those he meets, no matter that it may seem to be.

If you want more money, better health, or the state of marriage, Simon simply hears your desire as granted, then goes his way believing that what he has heard is now a physical fact which will confront you in the near future. He never seeks your thanks, but knows your desire must come into being; for he has lifted your burden upon his shoulder and believes in his own wonderful human imagination.

When you hear and believe in God's pattern of salvation, you are believing in Jesus. Everyone contains that pattern - therefore everyone is Jesus. Leave no one distressed. Do not give from your pocket, but give them every desire of their heart from your imagination. You could give money from now until the ends of time, and not give of yourself! Only when you imagine for another are you truly giving of yourself; and as you believe in the reality of what you have imagined, are you lifting the burden you are called upon to do, thereby fulfilling the law of God.

When you feel the joy of having done it, don't wait for the phone to ring; simply go your way and lift the burden from another, and then another. An artist friend recently told me about some work he had done for a friend, but had not been paid according to their verbal agreement. After our discussion I heard my friend tell me the debt was paid. That was all I did. Last night he told me that, seemingly out of the blue, the man came to his house and gave him a check for the full amount agreed upon. Now I will say to him that check will be multiplied over and over again, for there are many artists needing your talent to improve theirs.

Don't say something cannot be done, for the minute you do, you are placing a limit upon yourself. And don't limit your friend because of his financial, social, or intellectual background. That's a heavy cross for him to bear. Rather, lift his cross and set him free. We live in a world of horrors, but as Blake said: "Don't be intimidated by the horrors of the world. All is ordered and correct and must fulfill its destiny in order to attain perfection. Follow this pattern and you will receive from your own ego a deeper insight into the eternal beauties of reality. You will also receive an even deeper release from all that now seems so sad and terrible."

When you know this truth, you will lift the burden of all those you meet, for you will know that regardless of the pigment of his skin, the tongue in which he speaks, his belief, or nationality - you and he are one, for God is one. The great Sh'ma of the Hebrew confession of faith "Hear O Israel, the Lord our God, the Lord is one," will take on new meaning.

If God is one, there cannot be another; so, in the end you and I will be the same father of the same son. I have been sent to convey that one thought to the world. I have taught it through the spoken word and recorded it in my book, Resurrection, that God's true son is David. I have now completed the work I was sent to do.

The priests do not know the mystery. They are men without vision, reading a book they do not understand. To my mother, a priest was a wise man who could not be contradicted. I never argued with my mother about that, but I knew she was wrong. As a boy I had visions and knew the priests did not know what they were talking about; but mother could not understand how her little, uneducated boy could challenge that which she considered the wise men, because they could speak Latin and read Greek. But I knew their knowledge came from study, while my wisdom came from vision.

Having matured, I have been called and sent to reveal the true Son of God who unifies humanity. We will all know that one son to be our own son, for he will reveal each one of us as God the Father. Jesus Christ in you is God the Father, and David (in you) is His son. The day will come when David will awaken in you, rise in you, and call you Father, giving you a certainty which cannot be denied. Maybe from what you have heard tonight you may change your belief, but you will never know the certainty of Fatherhood until you see David as your son. And when everyone sees David as his son, are we not the one Father?

Tonight, I urge you to play the part of Simon. If you do, you will not be neglecting but helping yourself; for as told us in the story of Job, as he prayed for his friends his own captivity was lifted. While locked in his own desire to free himself of his physical, social, and financial problems, Job forgot himself and prayed for his friends, and in so doing all that he had lost returned to him one hundred-fold. As you pray for your friends you will discover your own captivity is lifted; your cross becomes lighter and lighter until finally you are light itself. So take my yoke upon you and learn from me, for my yoke is easy and my burden is light. Ask for no thanks or financial gain in the doing; just know the joy of lifting the cross, for it is being lifted from your own shoulders. When I hear that a man's needs have been provided for and he has become self-persuaded, it is true and it becomes true. I never tell him what I did. I simply revel in the joy and satisfaction of seeing this law of Christ fulfill itself. It never fails when put into practice.

Believe in the reality of your own imaginal acts, for faith is loyalty to unseen reality. Have faith in your imaginal act. Although unseen by the outer world as an external fact, your loyalty to its unseen reality will cause the unseen to become seen by the world. This is the practical side of this night. You and I can lift the cross from our own shoulders; for as I lift your cross I am lifting mine, and in a way, I do not know the burden is lifted from me. Everyone you meet is yourself made visible, for there is nothing but yourself in the world.

As you read these passages I have quoted tonight, pull them together and you will have a beautiful mosaic. Remember, when you do it to one of the least of these you have done it unto me, the one the world is seeking. You may see me as an insignificant little man, but I am Christ, the Lord God Jehovah. Lift my burden for even the most insignificant other, and go your way. You may not recognize your harvest, as you may not remember the favor you granted another many years ago. Seeing him healthy and financially secure today you may forget what you did, and maybe even he will have forgotten he ever asked your help - but what does it matter? The burden has been lifted. Go forward and play the part of Simon, and the day when you least expect it you will find the symbol of your creative power as a child wrapped in swaddling clothes. And then the 53rd chapter of Isaiah will be fulfilled, as your arm of God is revealed.

When scripture unfolds within you, you will know a thrill that is beyond ecstasy. Then you will no longer see scripture as secular history. You will know from experience that the story is supernatural, and has nothing to do with history as we understand it. The events spoken of by the apostles did not take place on earth, but in the soul of man as he walks the earth.

I have shared with you that which took place in my soul in the hope that I will find a few who will believe me to the point of putting my words into practice. I have unveiled myself to those who believe, and now they are beginning to be unveiled - while the rabbis and the priests who see me as an impostor remain veiled. Even to this day, when Moses is read the veil is on their minds. I pray for all of them because they are blinded to the truth by their refusal to accept any change in their fixed belief. I have come to do one thing: to make clear to the entire world who the true Son of God is who will unify the world.

Jesus Christ is God the Father and his son is David. When David calls you Father, you will know you are Jesus Christ, the Lord. If I am God the Father, who is my son? David. I tell you, David is not a physical being. It is in Spirit that he calls you Father, and scripture is fulfilled. Everyone will be called Father by the one being who is David, and if he calls you Father and he calls me Father, are we not the same being? Are we not the one God and Father of all? I tell you, without loss of your individual identity, you will know that you and I are one.

Now let us go into the silence.

Before Abraham, Was I Am

he drama tonight opens to the 8th chapter of the Book of John, where the evangelist writes of the state into which he has entered, saying: "Truly, truly I say to you, before Abraham, was I am."

The Bible is a recordation of the eternal spiritual states of the soul which everyone must pass through, beginning with the state of Abraham and culminating in the state called Jesus Christ. It is important, therefore, to distinguish between the man and the state he occupies at the present time.

Always remember that the Bible is address to the man of imagination and not to any mortal man. Blake said: "It must be understood that the persons Moses and Abraham are not here meant, but are states signified by those names. The individuals being representatives (or visions) of those states as they were seen by mortal man in a series of divine revelations and recorded in the Bible." I have seen these states in my imagination. At a distance they appeared as one man; however, as I drew near they became a multitude of nations. One man - represented by multitudes and multitudes of men in harmony - appears as a single being. The ancients saw Him and believing in what they saw they prophesied of the ultimate state, and personified him as Jesus Christ.

No one knows the true authors of Matthew, Mark, Luke and John, but I can tell you, they were relating their own experiences when they put words into the mouth of a personification of this ultimate truth called Jesus. Turning to those who were present he said: "Your father Abraham rejoiced that he was to see my day. He saw it and was glad." Those who heard him said: "Why, you are not yet fifty years of age, and Abraham saw you?" And he replied: "Before Abraham, was I am." With that remark they took up stones and stoned him.

Now this was not a drama that took place in the secular world. The evangelist is telling the truth, however, for being in the state of Jesus Christ he knew he was the immortal being who was before Abraham. He knew he was God himself, the author of the play called life. This truth every child born of woman will know from experience.

Let us now turn to the Book of Galatians, which is the earliest book of the New Testament. The thirteen letters of Paul were written, distributed, practiced, and called the gospel at least twenty years before the gospels Matthew, Mark, Luke, and John were written. In it, Paul speaks of "my gospel," saying: "I did not receive it from a man, nor was I taught it, it came by revelation of Jesus Christ." Then he tells this story: "Abraham had two sons, one by a slave and one by a free woman. The son of the slave was born according to the flesh, the son of the free woman by the promise. This is an allegory: these two women are two covenants. The one who bears the child by promise is Jerusalem from above." This is the state called Sarah.

Paul states quite boldly here that the story of Abraham, Hagar, and Sarah is an allegory. And an allegory is a story told as if it were true, leaving the one who hears (or reads) it to discover its symbolic representation and learn its lesson. Hagar and Sarah symbolize two covenants, one bringing in slavery and one freedom.

My mother was not named Hagar and the chances are your mother was not either, but every woman who has a child - in the language of symbolism - is Hagar. The child may be born in a palace and his mother a queen. He may know enormous wealth and a life of ease, but he (or she) is still a slave. Whoever wears a garment of mortality must take care of it, for it assimilates and must expel, through some artifice, that which it cannot assimilate. Whether the garment be that of a queen or a scrubwoman, it enslaves its occupant. And no matter how strong the garment, it waxes and waxes until it reaches a peak and then it wanes and wanes and no one can stop its inevitable change and death. So, every child born from the womb of woman is a slave.

But there is another birth - a birth into freedom - which is essential, for unless you are born from above you cannot enter the kingdom of God. And the womb from which that birth takes place is the human skull, called Jerusalem from above.

Blake identifies Jerusalem from above with liberty, for after this second birth one is liberated. Having been placed into a world of slavery and death, the second birth is our victory over death. Everyone will be victorious ... but everyone! We came into this world of death, have fought the good fight, and will continue to fight it. We are running a race with our enemy, death, in which all will be victorious. Everyone will be resurrected. Everyone will be born from above and all will enter the kingdom of God.

Ask no man to describe the kingdom for you, as eyes have not seen, nor ears heard, nor has it entered into the hearts of men the things God has already prepared for those who enter that state. There are no images here on earth to aid you in trying to visualize that state, so let no man tell you he knows and can describe it to you, for it can't be done.

The New Testament begins: "The book of the genealogy of Jesus Christ, the son of David, the son of Abraham." If the story of Abraham is an allegory, then the end of the story - called Christ - must be an allegory, for it was established in the beginning that everything would bring forth after its own kind. A carrot seed contains within itself the capacity to become a carrot. An apple seed when planted will bring forth an apple tree, and so forth. So, if the origin of any story is an allegory, the end is an allegory. Not knowing how to read scripture, man believes it is secular history and worships states, making mental pictures of them, painting and even sculpturing them; yet every character recorded there is only the personification of a state.

Let me share an experience of mine with you. In my vision I came upon a man in his fifties, about six feet tall, and looking as though he had an infinite capacity of faith. I didn't have to ask his name, for I recognized him instantly. (Wisdom from above is without uncertainty. When you come upon these states in vision, you know who they are). The moment I saw him, I knew I was looking at the state called Abraham. He was standing erect, yet leaning somewhat against the trunk of what looked like an oak tree totally devoid of leaves. Its branches were curled and knotted, resembling the human brain. Twisted around the trunk of the tree was a serpent with a human face, bathed in wisdom and the symbol of the final state called Christ. Abraham was looking - not into space, but time, and I wondered what this wisest of all of God's creatures had whispered into his ear.

Paul personifies scripture by saying: "The scriptures foreseeing that God would justify the Gentiles, preached the gospel beforehand to Abraham." The scriptures must be personified in order to preach. So, three thousand years before the coming of Christ, Abraham was given a preview of God's plan of salvation in the form of the gospel. Therefore, Abraham rejoiced that he was to see my day; he saw it and was glad.

When I say "I" (or "my") I mean "we," for we are the gods who collectively form God. In the great play, God is fragmented and the one becomes the many. But before the state of Abraham we - in perfect unity - wrote the play for a divine purpose. We agreed to enter the world of death and completely forget who we are in order to make the play real. This we have done and we will return enhanced by the play, but we cannot stop half way or turn back, we must finish the race. Everyone will fight the good fight. Everyone will go to the end and keep the faith we began in the state called Abraham.

The tree I saw was a perfect symbol of the tree of life. In Blake's "Songs of Experience," he said: "The gods of the earth and sea sought through nature to find that tree. But their search was all in vain, there grows one in the human brain." That's where the tree of life is. Having been felled, its roots are inverted in the brain with its branches as man's nervous and circulatory systems. Man is the inverted tree, like the one you would see reflected in the still waters of a lake. Turned down into generation, that tree symbolized as man, will be turned up from generation to regeneration. On that day man is resurrected and returns, bringing back the fruit (the experiences) of this great play of decay and death.

So Abraham is not a person as you are, as I am, any more than Isaac, Jacob, David, and all the others are persons. They are personifications of the eternal states of the soul. So if the origin called Abraham and the fulfillment called Jesus Christ are an allegory, then the fruit (glorious as it is) is also an allegory. And you will reap it to return greater than the being you were when you came out from the Father and came into the world, and no one will be lost... not one.

In the kingdom, however, we will play different parts, just as we play them here. Although sharing one body, one Spirit, one Lord, one God and Father of all, there are ranks in the kingdom just as there are ranks in the army. Those who fill the stars of the crown do so not by merit, but by election - which remains a secret of the Most High. But remember: the least in the kingdom is greater than the greatest on earth. "I would rather be a doorkeeper in the house of the Lord than live in the house of the wicked." Well, a doorkeeper may be on the threshold, but he is in the kingdom. We are told that no one born of woman is greater than John the Baptist, yet the least in the kingdom is greater than he.

No matter how great, wise, strong, or handsome one is here on earth, he is less than the least in the kingdom of God. So, do not be concerned as to what part you play in the body of God, for the least part is greater than anything on earth. In the third great act of God's awakening, you reenter the kingdom violently to discover your position. Entering the body of the Risen Lord like a bolt of lightning, you are the cause of its reverberation, and your entrance denotes your position. There will be no menial parts there, for all will be a necessary part of the body of the Risen Lord.

So, before Abraham, was I am. That is God's name forever and by this name he shall be known by all generations. God preceded his play, so the evangelist is telling the truth when he says, before Abraham, was I am.

Dwell on the words I have given you tonight. Know how truly great you are, then allow everyone to play their parts perfectly. If someone tells you he wants to feel important, let him feel it. If he wants to make an impression, let him make it. He is playing a part in the world of Caesar and maybe he has to make that impression for a certain self-satisfaction as he passes through the state. If you look at a person spiritually you can see the spiritual state he is in and realize that while he is in the state, he is playing his part perfectly.

We are all immortal beings who pass through states until we reach the state of Jesus Christ, the state designating the end of the journey. And when you enter that state scripture unfolds in you, casting you in the role of the central character and you are awed and thrilled. Prior to that moment in time you would have thought it blasphemy to claim such divinity, but when it happens you can no more deny it than you can the simplest evidence of your senses. And having experienced scripture, you have fulfilled the only purpose of life and you know it.

All of the stories of the Bible are supernatural truths which take place in a remote region of the soul. A lady here tonight said: "As I examined a translucent box covered with skin, you appeared and began to peel transparent skin from your cheeks." She saw correctly. At the end of the journey the skin you wear - which was so responsive to the inner you, that you thought you were it - will be taken off, and your true identity revealed.

I have a little namesake in New Your City. His name is Neville Mark. I saw him a month before he was born and when I asked when he was coming on earth he answered quite innocently: "The tenth of November." A very dear friend of ours was pregnant at the time and expecting her child in December. I shared my experience with her and told her that should her baby be born on the tenth of November and he was a boy, his name was Neville Mark. Well, even though she did not believe me, her baby arrived on the tenth of November and she named him Neville Mark. About three or four years ago I visited the family, and Neville Mark - twelve or thirteen at the time - said to me:

"Neville, I know that I am not what I appear to be. If I could only get my body to stand perfectly still while I turn around in it, I would know who I am. I also know I cannot do it until I die, and I can hardly wait to learn my true identity."

This little lad knew what my friend saw, for he knew that the skin which was tightly woven over him hid his true identity. This is true, for everyone here is wearing a mask. One day the mask will be taken off and we will all meet unmasked, yet we will know each other as we did before Abraham. There will be one grand, wonderful, joyous moment when- having returned - we recognize the being we were prior to putting on our masks to play the play of life.

The evangelist knew from his own experience that before the state called Abraham was I am, yet those who heard his story took up stones to throw at him. Now, a stone symbolizes a literal fact. The stones they threw were the facts of his life here on earth. They knew his parents, his brothers and sisters, as well as his educational and social background. They knew he was not yet fifty, yet he was speaking of one who was recorded to have lived two thousand years ago.

Friends here have thrown the same facts at me. I recall one night at a dinner party I told the late Aldous Huxley that these characters were not persons, and he said: "Neville, Caesar and Herod lived and they are mentioned in scripture" And I replied: "I speak of the scripture which is the Old Testament, and they are not there. If you want to accept Jesus as a man, the only book he could have read was the Old Testament. In the temple he was given the book and read the words of the prophet Isaiah. Everything he quoted was from the Old Testament, as the New hadn't been written."

I am not denying that Paul and the evangelists lived, but they are anonymous. The Old Testament is a recordation of eternal states, and the prophets who recorded them were doing a work the full import of which they did not understand. They inquired as to what time or person was meant, and it was revealed to them that they were serving not themselves, but us.

When the time fully comes, the secret will be uncovered and we will see the end, as we fulfill the state called Jesus Christ. Each will enter it, one after the other, and all will experience everything that is recorded in the scripture concerning Jesus Christ. And when each one of us has had the identical experience, who are we? Are we not Jesus Christ, the perfect man who reflects the glory of God and bears the very stamp of his person!

When you reach that state the work is done and you return to where you were before your deliberate fall. You did nothing wrong, but took the challenge, for only God could die in confidence that he would rise. We are the gods who took the challenge, who came down and entered these masks that decay and die, to find ourselves restored, waxing once more, waning, and dying. Restored, waxing, waning, and dying, over and over and over until the end is reached. Then there is no more restoration - only resurrection - as we are lifted out of the world of death to enter the kingdom of heaven, the world of life.

Everyone is destined to be in that kingdom, to play his predetermined part, for "Those whom he foreknew he predestined to be conformed to the image of his son, and those whom he predestined he called, and those whom he called he justified, and those whom he justified he glorifies." Everyone, even the least in the kingdom, will be glorified in the body of the Risen Lord and remember: before Abraham, was I am.

Now let us go into the silence.